SISTER EM

THE

# ROSARY

*A Journey That Changes Your Life*

children
of
Medjugorje

Ordering Information:
Orders by trade bookstores and wholesalers.
Please contact Ingram Content at www.ingramcontent.com.

ISBN-13: 978-1-7359106-3-5 (PAPERBACK)
ISBN-13: 978-1-7359106-4-2 (KINDLE E-BOOK)
ISBN-13: 978-1-7359106-5-9 (EPUB E-BOOK)

10 9 8 7 6 5 4 3 2 1

Available in E-Book.

www.childrenofmedjugorje.com
USA: 2400 E. Main Street, 103-156,
St. Charles, IL 60174, USA

# Contents

# The Luminous Mysteries

# The Sorrowful Mysteries

# The Glorious Mysteries

# Mysteries of Compassion

# Mysteries of Mercy

# Appendix

217

# Introduction

HY, ON CHRISTIAN RADIO stations, is the Rosary prayer the show with the largest audience?

Why, in CD sales charts, is the Rosary the bestseller?

Why did the great miracle-worker Padre Pio always have the Rosary in his hand?

Why did Mother Teresa of Calcutta's Rosary open all the doors for her?

Why does the Woman Who Crushes the Serpent's Head recommend the Rosary so much?

Why was the Rosary the favorite prayer of St. John Paul II?

Why does Satan tremble at the simple name of Mary in the Rosary?

Why is the Rosary the prayer of the New Times?

There is certainly a fundamental reason why Our Lady, in her messages, continually emphasizes the importance of praying the Rosary every day. What is the reason for this tender plea which she unceasingly demands from all of us? As a Mother, she knows the best way to lead her children to happiness. Many people have never prayed this prayer, many don't even know it, while others became bored and just gave up. I must say that the hidden treasure of the Rosary is not that easy to find, therefore I want to present to you my thoughts on the matter. There are two ways to pray the Rosary, the good way and the bad way, or rather we could say one is powerful and the other is weak.

The weak way—here is the scenario: I am deeply worried because one of my parents is dying in hospital and suffering terribly. I decide to pray a Rosary for my intentions, hoping to obtain his healing or at least some tangible alleviation of his pain. So, I start to say my Hail Mary's without thinking, with my spirit focused on the sufferings of this person, thinking of how I should deal with the whole situation. It goes without saying that once I have finished praying this Rosary I will be even more exhausted and worried than I was at the start. It's a shame because I actually devoted some of my time to it!

Here is the powerful way to pray the Rosary, which Our Lady has been teaching us with her motherly love since 1981. It's the same scenario: one of my parents is dying in hospital and experiencing excruciating pain. I am going to share all my worries with Our Heavenly Mother. Instead of getting stuck on the problem, I will let it go, I will throw it in to her Immaculate Heart and I will say to her "Now, Mother, it is YOUR problem! This burden is too heavy for me, you take care of it because you are my mother; are you not omnipotent in the Heart of the Lord? I will never refuse your grace! While You are dealing with my problem, my relieved heart will be free to pray with trust, love and peace".

This trustful prayer will allow me to focus on Jesus and to contemplate Him in the different episodes of His life on which we meditate each mystery of the Rosary.

# The Joyful Mysteries

How wonderful it is to begin our journey with Mary into the life of Jesus! The prayer of the Rosary leads us on an adventure during which we will discover unexplored landscapes and vast expanses that the eyes of our hearts could not imagine exist. Along the various mysteries, Mary will present to us her family album, pictures of the most beautiful of families. She will unveil for us the path followed by her Son and the most endearing events of His life. Let's enter her innermost thoughts, pausing at the important steps of her first years with Jesus, so that we can comprehend and absorb avidly every little bit of this pure, divine joy! Nothing will escape us, because our hearts, weary of the fickle joys of this world, ardently desire the source of living water, which will help them taste true joy.

Oh, Mary, our hearts are ready. Take us by the hand, guide us, and help us to discover your joy!

# The Annunciation

ET'S GO TOGETHER TO Israel, to the little town of Nazareth. An unknown young girl by the name of Myriam, often called Mary, lives here. I am a young child barely three years old. Now, at three years of age, children can be great mystics. With the typical ease of a child, I slip secretly into Mary's room, and what do I see? A beautiful young girl around fourteen years old. I must admit, I'm fascinated. Irresistibly drawn by the beauty and gentleness which emanates from her, I run towards her and cuddle up in her arms. With my little child-like antennae, I have understood everything: I am aware of the opening up of her heart and the tenderness pouring out.

You know children: they pick up everything! They understand immediately if they are welcome and wanted, or if we are tired of them and prefer that they leave us alone. In this case, the moment she saw me on her doorstep, I felt that she was happy to see me! Oh, I feel so good in her arms! I delight in her beauty and in a tenderness I've never experienced before. So, I snuggle up against her even more. I take her hand and I am quiet. I've never felt so comforted. There's no need to talk and there's no point telling her where I come from or

who I am. I'm simply a child! Holding her hand, I feel all the
peace which lives in her heart, a peace which flows through
me like a river and fills me up. I decide to never let go of the
hand of this Lady!

Little Jacinta of Fatima was also overwhelmed the first
time she saw the Blessed Mother. She was barely six years
old. After the apparition, she never stopped repeating: "Oh,
how beautiful she is, this Lady! How beautiful she is!" That's
all she could say, and, in so doing, she said it all!

I too while in Mary's room say the same thing: "How
beautiful this Lady is!" I remain at her side and squeeze tightly
against her; I sense that her peace nourishes me. I have such
a vital need for it!

It's unbelievable, but I have arrived at just the right
moment: it's the Annunciation! (LK 1:26-27) An angel has
arrived unexpectedly to surprise her and is beginning to speak
to her. Obviously, he is announcing to her some important
news! Since my hand is in hers, I can feel her trembling with
all her being, shaken by a strong emotion. Mary has just
learned that God has chosen her to be the mother of the
Messiah. How can she not be shaken? Among all women, it
is she whom the Father has chosen to become the mother of
His only Son, of the long-awaited Messiah. The one who is
going to save the world. The whole history of the world is
about to change dramatically! Feeling her hand tremble, I am
myself overflowing with joy, and my heart is beating wildly.

Using the eyes of my soul, I contemplate the Child Jesus,
Who is coming to curl up in the womb of this Immaculate
Virgin, through the action of the Holy Spirit.

Oh, how happy the infant Jesus is! He has waited for this
impatiently, and the day has finally come! Mary is saying her

YES, and now He's coming; there He is, He's arrived! He has pitched His tent among us, and He leaps for joy in the womb of His mother. The first hurdle has been cleared, and He can finally save us! Love is burning inside Him!

While praying this decade with all my heart, I allow myself to be invaded and impregnated by the joy of Jesus; I will absorb the joy from Christ Himself, from Jesus as a little embryo. It's difficult for us to imagine the depth of this reality. A God who makes Himself man! He, who is pure spirit, assuming our human nature. Out of an abundance of love, He wants to be like one of us, in order to live in the heart of our wounded humanity. He can't resign Himself to the idea of leaving us alone and exiled on this earth.

I am equally aware of the joy of the Father and of the Angel Gabriel when they hear this YES, so deeply hoped-for since the rebellion of man in the Garden of Eden. Feeling happy and content, I close my eyes; I will recite the Hail Mary, and Mary will reveal to me her most precious treasure, her Son, Jesus! Now, my heart is totally united with the heart of Mary. In her arms I allow myself to become enriched with her tenderness, for the greater glory of God. I open my heart as never before to let all these treasures penetrate me and to allow me to share them.

Now let's pray one *Our Father*, ten *Hail Mary's* and one *Glory Be*.

# The Visitation

E HAVE JUST LEFT Nazareth, and we are heading to the little village of Aïn Karim where Elizabeth and Zechariah live. I am still that little child of three years old, who holds the Blessed Mother's hand and doesn't for the life of me want to let it go. That image makes me think of what Mother Teresa of Calcutta, at eighty years old, recounted to a friend: "When I was five or six, I used to work in the fields with my mother. One day, we had left the house to go to another village a little farther away. I held my mother's hand, full of confidence, because I was aware that she knew the way perfectly. All of a sudden, she stopped in the middle of the road and said to me in a serious manner: "My daughter, you are entirely confident, you feel assured, right? You trust me, for you know that I know the way and that with me you will never get lost. Later in your life, when I am no longer here, do the same with your Mother in Heaven, the Mother of God! Keep your hand in her hand, and don't let go! It is she who will guide you and lead you to Jesus, to Heaven." And Mother Teresa added: "I have always followed my mother's advice, and today, I don't regret it. Our Lady has always guided me and never abandoned me!" As for us, if we happen to let go of Mary's hand at any time throughout the day, the Rosary furnishes us with the perfect opportunity to grasp it again and hold on tightly, so as never to let it go.

As we walk along together, I notice that Mary bears within her a great mystery: God Himself lives inside her. She has been a mother for just a few days. She hurries; she has just enough time to find a caravan to get to Aïn Karim, Elizabeth's village, after the Angel's announcement. So, she leaves with all the alacrity of love.

What is Mary feeling? Some women have told me that they felt a radical change in themselves the moment they found themselves pregnant. A friend confided to me that in the first months of pregnancy she became much more aware of her body. She was more protective of it, taking care not to make any sudden movements. Even at home she felt that her body no longer belonged to her alone, but also to a little defenseless infant growing inside her. Mary, the pure, the immaculate one, was even more sensitive to this presence.

From Nazareth, the road to Aïn Karim is long. Mary must have journeyed 180 kilometers, over five days of travel. I travel with her as well, very happy for this extraordinary experience! I'm hoping to figure out the big mystery, which is visible as she walks along the path, completely immersed in prayer, totally within herself, as though enveloped in peace.

The fact that a mother can carry a tiny human being in her womb has always been a great mystery. Today, psychologists know and can assert: from the moment of conception, when the baby has just implanted himself in his mother's womb, his body is miniscule, but his soul is already entirely present. A "baby soul" doesn't exist. That child already possesses innately a "conscience of love" which is an integral part of his soul.

The Holy Spirit has confirmed this also, through the prophets. This conscience of love, which is extremely sensitive, doesn't depend on the age of the body. But since the child has just come from the hands of the Creator, its soul is a sounding board, as profound as it is delicate: the child can already suffer intensely or feel great joy. Because he has a conscience of love, he picks up the emotions of his mother: whether she is feeling good or bad; whether she accepts the life she carries or rejects it; whether she is living her femininity in a good way, or if there's a problem in that area. A child is extremely sensitive to the spiritual and emotional life. He understands immediately whether, in the little tabernacle where he will live for nine months, peace or agitation will reign, love or hatred, bitterness or gentleness, fear and anguish or serenity. He even perceives whether a previous pregnancy was peaceful or if there was an abortion.

Certainly, he doesn't yet have enough brain cells to think, but he feels all this profoundly, and a great deal more than we imagine, thanks to the antennae of his soul! It is therefore fundamental that from the moment she is aware of being pregnant the mother protects the soul of her child. It is sufficient that she welcomes him with love, talks to him, prays with him, and, especially, that she already considers him a little person, fragile, perhaps, but very real; that she give him all the happiness and love he needs. By doing so, she helps him to grow in the harmony the Creator placed in him and she promotes his future well being.

We understand, then, how important it is that the mother and father maintain an atmosphere of peace in the center of the family and cultivate a climate of joy and tranquility during the entire pregnancy. The little embryo perceives very well the expectation of the mother and her enthusiasm for this new life unfolding in secret!

Now, let's pause, and, still holding Mary's hand, imagine the first dialogue which springs up between Mary and her Son. What an incredible exchange of love! We will only become familiar with it all in Heaven. Can we ever reproduce such a dialogue between a mother full of love and her little one who is Love itself? What a mystery! What grandeur! What an extraordinary relationship, starting right at that moment! And I, walking next to them, am drawn into this relationship. I feel genuinely concerned, because Mary has a message for me. Basically, she feels the same maternal love for me and for each one of us, the same infinite tenderness that she has for the Infant Jesus. Mary, who has carried the Child-God in her womb, loves all her children with the same intensity, nothing less!

As Saint Bernard of Clairvaux puts it, *"When we are on earth, we are not yet born. We are born when we* enter Heaven. On earth, we are carried in the womb of the Mother of God."

Our journey continues, and we finally arrive at Zechariah's house. I hear Mary greet Elizabeth in a way that is so touching! Elizabeth's entire being is uplifted at the greeting of Mary, her little cousin: a current of joy passes through her! Not the purely human joy of someone who sees a dear member of the family again . . . A joy entirely divine, that same joy the apostles experienced on the day of Pentecost, a joy which liberates the heart and makes you proclaim the name of God. In an instant, Elizabeth became a prophet. Saint Luke writes:

> "And it came to pass, when Elizabeth heard the greeting of
> Mary, that the babe in her womb leapt. Elizabeth was filled

with the Holy Spirit, and cried out with a loud voice, saying,
"Blessed art thou among women and blessed is the fruit of
thy womb! But why am I so favored that the mother of my
Lord should come to me? For, behold, the moment that
the sound of thy greeting came to my ears, the babe in my
womb leapt for joy." (Lk 1: 41-44)

But who, through Mary's greeting, received the Holy Spirit
first? Elizabeth or her baby? You know, don't you, it was the
infant John! But how can an infant perceive the presence of
God before his mother does? In the womb of Elizabeth, he
saw nothing, heard nothing . . . But he knew! The antennae
of his conscience of love vibrated! What a beautiful confirmation of those special antennae of the very young which
allow them to welcome the Holy Spirit before we, "the grown
ups," do! How very much we should respect these little ones
cherished by God, to whom the Kingdom of God belongs
first of all! Saint Elizabeth and her son were, from that day
on, filled with the Holy Spirit. John's mother, she who carries
the greatest of prophets and the Voice which will cry out in
the wilderness, will be the first to pronounce the words of the
second part of the Ave Maria that we, too, recite. That is the
power of Mary's visit to Elizabeth, who carried Jesus in her
womb! Mary always brings us Jesus and with Him, divine joy!

During this decade, which I'm going to pray with all my
heart, I'm going to allow myself to be engulfed in this immense
maternal love which comes upon me. What's going to happen
to me? It's possible that I was damaged in my mother's womb,
since I'm the eighth, maybe even the tenth child; or, perhaps,
my mother was sick when she conceived me, and she mur-
mured: "Oh, no, now's not the right time!" It's possible that

my father beat her or that he left with no forwarding address, or that my mother's financial circumstances were catastrophic . . . In short, my arrival wasn't opportune, and she perhaps thought of aborting me. I don't want to enumerate here all the possible scenarios, but let's think about it: if the mother doesn't comprehend the great gift which is life, what will the consequences be for the child? He will suffer rejection from the mother and will conclude that his life isn't worth much. He will perceive the risk of being expelled from his little hiding place like something that shouldn't be there. He will feel that his presence is an error and will therefore suffer a deep wound.

Let's think about this little one: he has only his mother to love him during this phase of his existence, and how he needs her! It could be me, this infant traumatized by a lack of love or rejection! It's possible that my own mother was afraid and that her anguish overwhelmed me. So, I took refuge in a corner of this little tabernacle, with no desire to see the day, preferring, perhaps, to die and never be born. It would be inevitable, then, that this trauma, of which I have no conscious memory, had repercussions in my adult life. For example, the impossibility of engaging in a normal relationship with others, homosexuality, deep-seated fears of amounting to nothing, the refusal of food or compulsive eating, fear of the future, psychological problems, problems at school, a series of failures, fear of getting married, or even sexual disorders, which greatly afflict this generation. For God is love and He is life. In Him these two attributes blend into one reality. Now, my mother was chosen to collaborate in my creation — she is co-creator with my Creator. If she gives me life without giving me love, she causes a deep wound in me.

But I will entrust to Mary my relationship with my earthly mother. I can offer her everything that I've experienced. From her hands, I will accept everything, and she will embrace me as she did with Elizabeth and her child! Mary will be very happy to satisfy me with whatever I lack, to make up for anything I missed! She will cure me of frustration. She can, basically, appease, calm, and relieve all the pain and violence anyone has endured! That's the power of Mary's visit.

In Medjugorje, she told us the secret of undertaking our inner healing: "Dear children, just as I carried my Son Jesus in my womb, I want to carry each of you along the path to holiness." She also told Jelena's prayer group: "Dear children, I love each of you as much as I love my Son Jesus." Incredible! So, nothing is lost for me; I can still get to know that maternal love that I have always desired so fervently. Mary gives me all her motherly tenderness, the same tenderness that she had for her little Jesus, nothing less! It is this pure, unalloyed tenderness which will heal me completely. The specialty of the Mother of God is to fill that emptiness in my heart that makes me suffer deeply; to cure me of the frustrations that the Evil One has injected in me to remove the little peace I had. Basically, the Evil One is "frustrated by excellence", as Saint Teresa of Avila used to say, and he wants to inoculate us with his mortal venom.

Maybe I was a victim of a lack of love and attention in my childhood, but is it possible that I myself did not show love to my own children? Maybe I aborted or helped another mother abort or gave in to the blackmail of my baby's father, who refused life. It's possible that I forced my daughter to abort by saying: "You're only fourteen years old. It's too soon to have a child, and we don't want any problems in the family

. . ." And even if the young mother didn't want to kill her baby, parental pressure obligated her to give in. Obviously, I am also speaking about fathers.

I will allow myself to heal day by day, and that way will bring great joy to my Heavenly Mother. She came to me with the sole purpose of giving me her Son who erases sin and who saves, just as she did by visiting Elizabeth. With Mary, I will praise and magnify the Lord, the Most-High, because He has accomplished marvelous things in my life. I am also blessed that Jesus has saved me, and that I will be with Him for all eternity.

Over the course of this decade, I will close my eyes and once again become a little baby. I will permit my Heavenly Mother to achieve a miracle, to visit me in the most secret recesses of my being. Here I'm going to suggest praying to the Child Jesus, still hidden in the womb of Mary.

O, dear little Child Jesus, curled up in the womb of your Immaculate Mother, I come to pay you a visit. I need to talk to you. I need to tell you first how much I marvel that God in person took on our flesh, so fragile and vulnerable. You made a dizzying leap from the celestial splendor you lived in with the Father to espouse our truly miserable human race and to take on with us all the risks . . . that compels me to adore you. How can I not love You? How can I not cherish You infinitely as a zygote, an embryo, as a fetus, as a child not yet born, before even discovering Your face in the poor stable in Bethlehem! Yes, I love You, because You did that out of pure love for me, for my family, for all of humanity. You came into our lowly mire to save us, to elevate us towards You, and to offer us the delights of eternal life in Your presence.

You alone, Jesus, could imagine such folly! But You haven't finished surprising us!

Jesus, You know, my visit is a little self-serving, don't be surprised! Today there are millions of miniscule beings like You hiding in the wombs of their mothers! Their angels in Heaven never stop contemplating the face of Your Father Who is in the Heavens. More innocent than they will never be found on earth. Jesus, you know that they've all received the gift of life, but all have not received the gift of love. Some swim in happiness feeling the love of their mothers, but others ask themselves what on earth they are doing here, because they sense that they've been rejected.

Jesus, You are at once Life and Love. I beg you, visit them all! Visit the little ones who are jubilant to feel themselves loved, and visit, also, the others who suffer, because they have received life without love. You are so little that approaching them will not frighten them. On the contrary! Come, find them where they are, in these fragile tabernacles of human life, where they are slowly growing. You are the same size as they are, like their divine twin! Thanks to those extremely sensitive antennae their innocence bestows on them, they are completely attentive to the soul of their mother, and to their Creator. Take advantage of it, Jesus! Tell them that they are infinitely precious. Tell them how much You see in them Your own image, how much You are anxious to see them grow, to become fully what they are in Your plan of love!

And if they have to be torn away, naturally or with violence from their little hiding places, O, tender Jesus, listen to their cries of anguish, and pour into them Your immense love! Heal their wounds! May it be done to them according to Your will, Jesus: "Father, I will that where I am, they will be with me!" Let this outpouring of love envelop, as well, the hearts of those who have chosen to lose them, so that they throw themselves into Your arms of mercy.

O, tiny little Jesus, hidden in Mary, how can I thank You for having visited me in my mother's womb, when with my father, she consecrated me to Your Sacred Heart and to the Immaculate Heart of Mary! Help all parents to do the same; distance them from the wolves which want to carry off and devour the children of men!

O, little Jesus, hidden in Mary, listen to my poor prayer for those little ones like You. And on Christmas Day, come, be born in my heart; it yearns for You; it waits and watches for You in the night as a watchman waits for dawn! *Maranatha!*

Now let's pray one *Our Father,* ten *Hail Mary's* and one *Glory Be.*

# The Birth of Jesus in Bethlehem

AM STILL THAT LITTLE child, and I haven't left Mary's side for a second! Right now, we are in the stable in Bethlehem. I would be sad sitting in this pitiful refuge if I wasn't drawn to it by an unexpected phenomenon: the infant Jesus sleeping in an animal manger! When you are little and surrounded by giants, you are very happy to discover, at last, someone smaller than you. I move in close and, with great wonder, look at this little newborn baby in his manger. He can neither walk nor talk, as opposed to me, a big three-year-old! I look at this family in which there is infinite love. I did well to give my hand to Mary, thank God! Here I am now in the presence of a new-born and of his father and mother; I have found my family! There reigns in this stable such an intensity of love that Satan has never been able to put his feet down here; he has never been able to infiltrate the Holy Family: the love there is too strong! Let's contemplate the members of this very endearing family: Joseph, the righteous, full of tenderness, who loves Mary to death; Mary, the Immaculate Conception, completely selfless and loves Jesus to death; and the Child-God, Love itself, who loves the world to death. Let's imagine for a moment what a fire of love and tenderness unites them!

In Medjugorje, Our Lady invites our families to become like the family in Bethlehem. She says:

> "How happy we were, dear children, when my Son was born! May your families be as joyful as we were in the stable when my Son Jesus was born!" (To the prayer group, December 14, 1991)

During this decade, I will focus my attention on the Child Jesus, on His Holy Mother and on Saint Joseph, and I will let myself be transformed by this intensity of love! Let's open our hearts to the newborn Jesus by praying the following words:-

### PRAYER TO THE NEWBORN INFANT JESUS

O, Infant Jesus, I love You! I look at You and see You, so small, so innocent, so vulnerable . . . But You are my Lord and my God! Along with Mary, Joseph, and the shepherds of Bethlehem, I also come to adore You. May my heart become Your manger; come, live in me!

Little Jesus, Herod wanted to kill You, even though You came to save us. Throughout my life, save me from all sin and from any action which could offend You. Fill my soul with love and the divine peace to which I aspire so much.

Oh, I would so much love to take You into my arms, as Your mother Mary does, and cover You with tender kisses! You are cold in the winter of Bethlehem: I want the songs of my soul to warm You. May each action of secret love transform itself into a little bit of straw to contribute to Your comfort and to warm You.

Protect me from Satan; don't let him sow hatred and division in my family. Come, re-create love among us. May Your innocence destroy evil!

I beseech You, Infant Jesus, tend the wounds in my heart, and heal my illnesses.

Little Divine Shepherd, may Your blessing always be upon us! Guide us on the path of salvation!

At this moment, the Blessed Mother guesses my desire: she sees that I am irresistibly drawn to the Child. So, she takes Him in her arms, kisses Him, and, to my great surprise she puts Him in my little outstretched arms; she gives me her Child! I receive upon my heart the Child Jesus, newly-born, and I contemplate Him. She gave Him to me; she didn't lend Him to me! She has just brought Him into the world for me, to give Him to me as my Savior; she is giving Him to me for real. In Medjugorje, in a Christmas message, she tells us: "Dear Children, I came today with my Son, so that He might bless you," and in another message: "Dear Children, put little Jesus, the new-born child, in the first place in your life, and He will guide you on the road of Salvation." (DECEMBER 25, 1999) She offers Him to us so that we will put Him first in our hearts.

While reciting this decade of the Nativity, I will hold the Child Jesus tightly against my heart, so that I will receive great healing. If it is true that we become what we contemplate, then by contemplating the Newborn Jesus, what am I going to receive? All His innocence! Held against my heart, He can communicate to me His childlike spirit; where I am impure, complicated, or overly rational, my heart will fill up with love, with innocence, with beauty, because it will be He, the Child Jesus, who will give me those treasures.

But what does Mary mean when she invites us to put Him first in our lives?

First of all, I have to protect Him as a father and mother would. When you returned from the hospital with your newborn, didn't you turn everything upside down in the house and change your old habits? No more yelling, slamming of doors and heated discussions. This was replaced with gentleness and calm . . . Didn't the baby become the center of your thoughts? Every mother has a little watchdog inside her who makes her wonder: "What does my little one need now?" Faced with an infant, so tiny and so vulnerable, didn't you make his needs your priority?

That's what the Blessed Mother wants us to do with her Son, Jesus! She knows that if she entrusts Him to us as a newborn, we will have to take Him into our arms, carry Him with us, and watch over Him, because a baby is helpless without us. We will, therefore, make Him our priority and organize our lives according to His needs. Mary entrusts Him to me so that He will live with me and my life will be transformed!

I beg of you, take care of the Child Jesus in your arms, take care of Him all your life, not only during this decade. Press Him against your heart and ask: what does He need right now, my little Jesus? A newborn essentially needs three things: (1) Milk. Is He hungry? Well, then, I will feed the poor, because by nourishing the needy, it is Jesus whom I feed. (2) Love. I will try, then, to give love to all those around me, because "whatsoever you do to the least of my little ones, you do unto Me," (MT 25: 40) Jesus tells us. (3) The voice of his mother.

This simple, tender voice helps him to feel that he belongs to a family, to a group, so as not to feel alone and abandoned. This voice reassures him in his helplessness. It's the voice of the mother which forms him. A mother keeps repeating the same things and this regular repetition will provide him with a deep inner security. It will educate him little by little and help him to grow. How do I make him hear my voice? Through prayer! I will begin to pray, therefore, because praying means loving the Child Jesus, giving Him the attention that He needs, the time, the smile, the hug that He's craving for.

A newborn also needs to be caressed by gentle hands and to feel the maternal warmth which passes over his face; he needs to be touched, while hearing these tender little words from their mother! How can I caress the Child Jesus? By going out to the poor who need me, by caring for the ones who even lack the strength to beg. . .

Mary tells us: "He will lead you on the path of salvation." It is He, the newborn, our guide! We want to love Him so much! But it's not enough to say, "Oh, how cute and precious You are! How beautiful you are! How I love You!" because even the pagans used to speak that way. We need to love Him with divine love, with that love He longs for. But how can we love Him divinely? In Scripture, Jesus gives us the definition of the one who truly loves Him . . . *"He who has my commandments and keeps them, it is He who loves Me."* (JN 14:21)

Since He is our guide, we just have to follow Him. For example, if we have a choice to make or a decision to take, instead of consulting our friends, even astrologists, seers, or other people of that nature, let's join our hearts to Jesus' and ask Him, "Infant Jesus, what is Your will in this situation?

What do You think about it? What is Your plan?" Believe me, through deep prayer, He will answer you!

Mary tells us: "Dear Children, in a special way I call you: pray! For only through prayer will you be able to overcome your will and discover the will of God, even in the smallest things." (MARCH, 25, 1998)

The prophet Isaiah said: *"A little boy shall lead them."* (IS 11:6) Today, it is difficult to find good spiritual directors, so why not make the Child Jesus our guide? That's what Our Lady asks us to do in Medjugorje. I'm not saying that He will send us a message through WhatsApp or email, no! We shouldn't expect to hear His voice, but whatever our question, if we truly want to accomplish His will, He Himself, in a mysterious way, will orient our souls and minds in the right direction, towards His will. His greatest wish is for us to reach Heaven! Let's open ourselves up to His childlike spirit, to His tenderness, to His innocence; then we will allow ourselves to be illuminated by His presence! Have you noticed that even the toughest of men become tender and gentle when they take a newborn in their arms?

Do you want to find favor with Jesus? During this decade, whisper these words to Him and He will be delighted:

"Infant Jesus, from now on You will be my guide! When I have a choice to make, I will consult only You! I promise to follow You from this day on, to follow Your footsteps, to submit to Your inspirations. I love You and I will never abandon You again! I will always remain in Your embrace! Infant Jesus, I need You! You are my little star of Bethlehem!"

Now let's pray one Our Father, ten Hail Mary's and one Glory Be.

# The Presentation of the Child Jesus in the Temple

OU MIGHT HAVE NOTICED that with every decade we pray, we receive specific gifts from God? It's true, every decade brings new graces to us, and God gives them to us joyfully! What gift does God have in store for us during this Mystery? Before we discover it, I wish to repeat this: when we take the Rosary out of our pocket, let's squeeze it a little and remember that it's not a simple object, but it's really the hand of the Blessed Mother we grasp. Let's take her hand and be determined never to let it go again! When I hold the Rosary I am holding onto Mary!

We continue on our journey with the Holy Family, and from Bethlehem, we walk towards Jerusalem. Here we are in front of the Temple. What great majesty! I notice that Mary is walking next to Joseph, so that she can place the infant on the altar. I gaze at the scene, and what do I see? Mary presents her Son to God the Father. She received the gift of this Infant at a young age, and she could have said: "This is my Son, the special gift God gave me!" However, just as Abraham put

Isaac on the altar (that child, too, was a miraculous gift from God), Mary placed her Infant on the altar.

With the simple gesture, Mary lets her true love for Jesus shine through; she loves her baby with a divine love, and, for that reason, she will put herself entirely at His service, so that He can fully achieve His mission as Redeemer of the world. Out of love, she will sacrifice herself for Him. Jesus, the Infant that she carried to the Temple, has been called to become — and is already — the Redeemer of the world!

I marvel at the candor and the seriousness of Mary. She looks at me then invites me to come closer. I am standing now at the side of the altar, and, with all my heart, I welcome her invitation. Through her solemn gesture, I am learning what it means to love someone with a divine love. This moment is crucial for me. In Medjugorje, Mary tells us: "Dear Children, may love prevail in each of you! Not human love, but God's love!" (NOVEMBER 20, 1986) Divine love is one of oblation: it presupposes the gift of self; it focuses on the happiness of the one we love, the greatest happiness that could ever be destined for Him!

Mary didn't keep her Son for herself alone, as many mothers are tempted to do. The Presentation of the Son to the Father proves that Mary is entirely at the service of God's plan for the One she loves: that's divine love! She is prepared; she will continue until the very end, whatever the cost. Mary, the Seat of Wisdom, knows Scripture. She is acutely aware of the pain of the Suffering Servant, described by the prophet Isaiah. God, in His infinite goodness, wants everything we offer to be freely given; that is why he sends Simeon and Anna to tell Mary that this Infant is destined to accomplish great things, an immense mission in which she will have to support and accompany Him. She knows that He will receive neither honors nor gratification, but atrocious suffering, and *"thy own soul a sword shall pierce."* (LK 2: 35) Mary offers her Son in full knowledge of the facts, and she offers herself as well! To love in a divine way is to give your own life! *"Greater love than this no one has, that one lay down his life for his friends,"* affirms Jesus (JN 15:13). Through this, Mary gives us a beautiful example.

Our love is often turned towards a particular person: our child, our husband, our wife, our fiancé, or another; there is, frankly, someone I love more than all the others. Right now, I'm going to whisper his name to the Blessed Mother, and I will put this person on the altar, next to the baby Jesus. I will ask Mary for the grace to love this being in a divine way, not merely in a human way. We know very well what it means to be attracted to someone. The pagans themselves felt these attractions towards others like them. I recall a passage from Scripture heard rarely at church: *"Every plant that my heavenly Father has not planted will be rooted up."* (MT 15:13) What does that mean? Quite simply that all things originating in the flesh, from our earthly condition, even the best, will not enter into the Kingdom of Heaven, unless they are transfigured and made divine by the grace of God.

Certainly, nature is created by God, and we shouldn't hold it in contempt. We can't promulgate laws against nature, against Creation. Creation is wonderful, but all the same, it must be transfigured. Mary already possessed this divine love at the moment of the Annunciation. As for us, we need some time to learn to love the way God loves. I love in a human way when I am attracted to someone, when I feel good in his company, when that person brings me something; this type of love is very natural, indeed carnal. But the center of that sentiment is me! That emotion is certainly not a sin, but it won't lead us to the Kingdom of Heaven! On the other hand, when I'm seeking above all the happiness of the person I love, when I desire sanctity for him and do my best to help him accomplish God's plan in his life, then my love is divine! The central focus of this love is the other.

If the person I love most is my child, then I will help him become a saint with the help of Mary. Such is the plan of God for him, and He wants me to collaborate with it, because, in His great goodness, God trusts me. Or let's suppose that I am a married woman, very much in love with my spouse; I must do everything possible for him to become a saint, by sacrificing myself to attain this objective during our entire conjugal life. It is the same for fiancés. A young man might say: "Oh, how beautiful she is; she's the ideal woman I've been waiting for; we'll have children, buy a lovely house; I'll get a good job, so my family will lack nothing. . ." These considerations are good, but human! With Mary's help, I might learn to say instead: "Lord, use me, so that my spouse may become a saint, and so that we may form together a holy family." Such is the only love which endures forever. How long does purely human love last today? We see more than ever today how quickly it expires and fades away.

Let's return to the words of Mary: "Dear Children, begin by loving the members of your family, and then you will be able to love and accept all who come here." (DECEMBER 13, 1984) Let us pray now that, during this decade, divine love from the Holy Spirit will inflame our hearts and transform them.

Now let's pray one *Our Father*, ten *Hail Mary's* and one *Glory Be*.

# The Finding of the Child Jesus in the Temple

ET'S CONTINUE AGAIN ON our journey, but this time we don't need to go far, because we are once again at the Temple of Jerusalem. Jesus is about twelve years old when His parents find Him there after three days of anxiously searching for Him (LK 2:41-52). As for me, I never let go of Mary's hand, and I could feel her distress! Mary had not simply lost her only son — which would throw any mother into profound agony — but she had also lost her God! It's difficult to imagine the anguish the Blessed Mother experienced in those circumstances! The Greek word for "anguish" employed in the Gospel to describe Joseph and Mary's distress, is the same as that used to describe the agony Jesus experienced in the Garden of Gethsemane. Three days and three nights of futile searching; so many miles traveled in order to scrutinize every corner of their route, and He couldn't be found! These words from the Canticle of Canticles seem to have been written for that exact moment:

"I opened the door to my beloved; but he had turned aside and was gone. My soul melted when he fled: I sought him and found him not. I called, and he did not answer me." (Can 5:6)

When Joseph and Mary returned to the Temple, and, looked between two bearded rabbis, whom did they see? The little brown, curly head of dear Jesus! He was alive! He was really there! He seemed to her to be born anew, but in a totally different way. In that Temple no angels were singing the glory of God; the shepherds weren't there; there were no kings guided by a star; there were no miracles; the only people present were Joseph and Mary, who knew the true identity of that young adolescent. They were alone among the crowd who were curiously observing and judging them for having lost their son; alone with the stones of the Temple, and no angel to explain the meaning of those three days spent in anguish. That day Mary, who had never known the pains of childbirth, had just given birth to the Messiah. The anguish and the spiritual night of the soul she suffered then, had contributed to her heart being opened in completely new and extraordinary dimensions.

When suffering afflicts our hearts, what is our very gentle God the Father doing? If we accept the suffering and offer it up, He opens up our hearts, He increases our capacity to love and enables us to welcome divine love. Think about the saints who are already in Heaven or about those who have suffered enormously during their lives and who shine with love! Our capacity to love grows when we are in pain! That's why we gain everything by blessing the Lord for the suffering we've experienced, and, if we have not done so yet, let's offer it to Him right now, so that He may sanctify us.

During those distressing three days and nights, God prepared Mary to welcome Jesus in a new light! But what is so new about it? Jesus said: *"Did you not know that I must be about My Father's business?"* (LK 2:49) That's what has changed: the nature of the relationship between Jesus and His parents will never be the same. Jesus, drawn into the Temple by the Holy Spirit, leaves behind the warmth and support of his parents and becomes fully conscious of His mission as Redeemer. At age twelve, the age when boys become adults in Israel, the human soul of Jesus corresponds fully with the plan of the Father. Jesus abandons everything for the Father. He will affirm later: *"My food is to do the will of Him who sent me, to accomplish His work."* (JN 4:34) From then on, it's settled. But at what price! In His heart, Jesus feels the pain caused to his parents, whom He loves dearly.

Mary, on her part, understands that her Son has changed and has entered a new chapter in his life. She had to go through this suffering to be able to welcome this new face of Jesus. At that moment, the Father is revealing Himself more clearly to all three of them. Mary realizes that, through this detachment, the Father is already preparing her for the moment she will let go of her Son. She certainly remains His mother, but from now on, it is the Heavenly Father who will teach Jesus everything and will guide Him. She, along with her Son, will be subject to the plan of the Father. When Jesus turned twelve, her maternal authority diminished: it was the hour of the Father! And what about Joseph? What did he think when he heard Jesus talking about the business of His Father? Like Mary, through this agonizing trial, he is also preparing for this detachment so that he can adjust to this new dimension of his Son's life. It's a trial which makes him become even more humble!

As St. Luke relates, *"The child was obedient to them."* (LK 2:51) From then on, it was as though Mary had another Son. Returning to Nazareth, she held Him against her heart and prayed humbly. Even today, as in Bethlehem, facing this great mystery which is only partly revealed and not yet completely understood, she treasures all these events in her heart!

With this mystery, I too, like Mary, am in shock. In my life, I sometimes feel an emptiness, an absence, like a black hole! In Medjugorje, Mary is aware of this and tells us: "Dear Children, there is an emptiness in you; don't hang onto these voids!" She goes as far as affirming: "Dear Children, your hearts are hard and empty." Are we in that state right now? Who among us hasn't experienced these voids, these yearning gaps which still, perhaps, make us suffer? Who among us has never known a wound from love, an internal paralysis which prevents us from being joyful, from praising and adoring God, from knowing how to take a chance and taste peace?

What a gift has been given to us in this mystery of the Finding of the child Jesus in the Temple. Mary had to go through these three days of abandonment, so she could allow herself to be overwhelmed again by the presence of her Jesus. She hadn't lost Him in her heart, but she didn't have Him with her; He wasn't there physically. And then, all at once, there He was! Jesus came at that time to embrace the troubled heart of His mother, devastated by her loss.

And all of this will happen again for her! Several years later, Mary would nearly die of pain, facing the death of her Son. Her soul continued to search for Him, however she had to endure three more days of agony until the Resurrection! It all seems like a dress rehearsal for the heartache of those three days in the tomb. But even then, she would find Him again changed. To her, He appeared luminous and victorious. In Medjugorje, Mary tells us: "Dear Children, the Resurrection is always happening." She experienced it!

Throughout this decade, I, too, holding Mary's hand, will let her torrent of love for Jesus flow within me. I will open my heart wide to God, so that He might come to live there and allow me to bring Him back to my home, the way Joseph and Mary did. They set out with Him and "He was subject to them." I will go with them, starting today, with no feeling of emptiness or frustration. Jesus and the Holy Spirit will be present within me. I will become, like Mary, a living tabernacle.

Right now, I'm going to close my eyes and think in a particular way about the millions of brothers and sisters tormented by emptiness, tortured by an oppressive black hole in the depths of their souls, a hole they can't seem to fill. "Many young people are seeking happiness in the places where they lose it," Mary tells us. These young ones were, however, created in love and for love; how can they satisfy their great capacity to love? They are captivated by the mirages of this world. Many satisfy their interior emptiness with music, which overwhelms the ears and deafens the soul, with drugs, alcohol, harmful gaming, or even sexual deviations. And the parents no longer know what their children are doing. The poor souls are looking for anything to fill the void, yet all they find is a deeper, darker interior abyss. Only God can satisfy them. And the devil, always ready to profit by this void, is free to work. His task is easy because generally, his prey are souls who don't frequent the sacraments. He works, he corrupts, he ruins, he uses blackmail, and makes his victims slaves to the point of pushing them into despair; some even make a pact with Satan! Many prefer to die, because they believe only then will they be free from this void.

During this decade, I'm going to think about them, these young ones, and the not-so-young ones, and I will be like Mary, that tireless mother, who traveled many miles to find her Son that is lost. Through prayer, I will also guide those who do not yet know the love of God towards the full realization of the Father's design for their lives. That is one of the most important intentions of Mary's heart. From now on, not one day will pass by without me comforting our Mother's heart by praying for this intention.

On May 24, 1984, she revealed her suffering to us: "I beseech you not to permit my heart to cry with tears of blood, because of souls who are lost through sin." And on December 2, 2016, through the visionary, Mirjana, she declared:

> "Dear Children, my maternal heart cries when I see what my children are doing. Sins are multiplying and the purity of the soul is of less and less importance. My Son has been forgotten. He is seldom honored, and my children are persecuted."

These children feel an inner emptiness because no one has ever spoken to them about the love of God. Throughout this decade, I will remember all those young people who haven't been evangelized, and pray that God fill them with His love and that no person on earth suffer from an emptiness of the soul! We were all created for plenitude! "When you have God, you have everything!" Mary tells us (JULY 25, 1998). Those who have God are happy and already taste something of the happiness of Heaven. The visionaries Vicka and Jakov tell us how they saw Heaven.

Upon leaving the Temple of Jerusalem with Jesus, I take Mary's hand, and like her, I feel that wave of indescribable joy, because God is with me like never before: He is inside me!

Now let's pray one *Our Father,* ten *Hail Mary's* and one *Glory Be.*

# The Luminous Mysteries

ET'S CONTINUE OUR ROSARY with the Luminous Mysteries. At this point, I would like to quote a priest, who used to say: "When you take your rosary out of your pocket, imagine that you are taking Mary's hand! Hold it tight and never let it go! Walk with her, remain in her presence! Then your rosary will be said along with Mary, who is completely focused on Jesus!"

Basically, by praying the Rosary, we are calling to mind the mysteries of the life of Jesus and of Mary. Just as Mary's memory helps her re-live the life of her Son, let us, also, approach those blessed places and scenes with a child's heart. Let us be like children: nothing escapes their notice!

When we pray the Rosary, we are taking refuge under Mary's motherly mantle. She tells us: "Dear children, I want to hold you close to my heart and embrace you." She wraps us in her motherly cloak to protect us from the attacks of Satan. But what exactly is her maternal cloak? We certainly don't mean a coat she would use against the cold . . . no! Rather, it is the protective covering of the Holy Spirit received on the day of the Annunciation, when the Angel Gabriel said to her: *"The Holy Spirit will come upon you, and the power of the Most High will* overshadow you!" (LK 1:35)

When we nestle in Mary's cloak, the Holy Spirit shelters and protects us. Mary's cloak is God himself! That is why Satan has never been able to penetrate it with his poisonous ways.

When we pray the Rosary, let's not focus only on protecting ourselves under her mantle; let's take the whole world with us. We should bring with us all those we carry in our hearts and those whom we consecrate explicitly to the Blessed Mother: our dear ones, our friends, those who are undergoing trials . . . It is important that, in all families, there be at least one person who prays the Rosary for the purpose of placing the entire family under Mary's mantle. That is so powerful! Mary will always remember a family which prays the Rosary faithfully every day: an abundance of blessings will come upon all its descendants from generation to generation.

With the Rosary, we enter into the sheltering tent of Mary; we join with her in the intimacy of her room. Let's live there with her!

# The Baptism of Jesus in the River Jordan

**W**E ARE IN THE desert of Judea, on the banks of the Jordan: a huge crowd has assembled around John, the forerunner, to receive a baptism of penance: everyone confesses his sins. That's when a certain man arrives: Jesus of Nazareth! He comes forward to ask for baptism, just like all the others. John recognizes him immediately. It's his cousin! He knows that Jesus is the Lamb of God, the one who takes away the sins of the world. So dumbstruck, he says: "It is I who need to be baptized by you, and yet it is you who come to me?!"

It is important to note that in the Old Testament, "the waters" were often symbolic of the dwelling place of demons a deep, shadowy place, the home of evil. Let's take, for example, Psalm 69: "Save me, O God! For the waters have come up to my neck. I sink in deep *mire, where there is no foothold. I have fallen into deadly waters, and the flood sweeps over me.*" The power of the waters is the power of evil, which can sweep over us at any time, preventing us from living and from seeing the light. At the time John was baptizing, the Jordan was rife with all the sins of those who came to confess.

At that time, as a sign of purification, people were completely immersed in the water at baptism. When people resurfaced, only their sins remained in the river. Jesus was also plunged into the water when baptized by John. But it doesn't make sense! He is utterly pure; He has no need! So, why does He do it? Jesus plunges into the waters, because He plans to sanctify the waters; he's going to visit in his divinity the dark places of humanity. *

Jesus plunges into the waters, because he wants to take our sins upon Himself, by wrapping himself in them as he would a cloak! St. Paul affirms: *"For our sake, He made him to be sin who knew no sin"* (2 COR 5:21). Jesus takes the sin in order to expiate our sin. He, the Pure, the Holy, the Immaculate has taken upon Himself, upon his body, our sins, without ever having committed a single one. In a sense, He clothes Himself in them, so that three years later, those sins can be nailed with Him on the cross and, therefore, vanquished. At his own baptism, Jesus already sees the cross: from now on, He will live his public life with these invisible articles of clothing, before being raised from the dead to destroy death on its own terrain. Because *"the wages of sin is death."* (ROM 6:23)

At the moment of His baptism by John, Jesus inaugurates His ministry as Redeemer, by identifying with our sin. "It is fitting that we do this to accomplish all justice." But what

---

*    Even today, there is no need to have the water of the Jordan blessed when it is carried back home; it has already been blessed by the immersion of the Son of God!

does justice have to do with this scene? It's certainly not a matter of human justice but of divine justice, which is, simply put, mercy. In short, in God's plan, it was necessary for the Son to make Himself sin in order to nail our sin to the cross, and, therefore, to vanquish it: that is God's justice, completely woven of mercy. And Jesus adheres entirely to God the Father's merciful plan.

During this decade, I'm going to think about my own Baptism, which made me a child of God. On that day, Jesus took away my sin, while I was clothed with his eternal life. I received the white robe of renewed purity. What a great exchange! God alone could have conceived of it! Through Baptism, I was able to experience Christ's death and resurrection, so that I could clothe myself again with Him. My sin was vanquished, thrown into the sea, finished and forgotten. In an abundance of love, God forgot about evil!

I propose that you re-live the grace of your Baptism and that you repeat together those marvelous promises, especially if you were baptized as babies. There is great power in doing this! Many exorcists have confirmed it: if you have become enmeshed with Satan in some way, if he presses you, attacks you, assails you and tries to seduce you, re-read in a heartfelt way the promises of Baptism, and Satan will let you go. The recitation of these promises is the best exorcism that a lay person can do.

Now, answer the questions from our rite of Baptism to obtain the liberty of becoming a child of God. ··

---

·· The Church assures us of the indulgences to the faithful who renew the promises of Baptism in such a rite. In particular "A plenary indulgence is accorded to the faithful who in the celebration of the

In order to live in the freedom of the children
of God, do you reject sin? *I do.*

In order to escape the power of sin, do you
reject those who lead you into evil? *I do.*

In order to follow Jesus, do you reject Satan
who is the author of sin? *I do*

Do you believe in God, the Father Almighty,
Creator of heaven and earth? *I do.*

Do you believe in Jesus Christ, His only son our Lord, who was
born of the Virgin Mary, suffered death and was buried, was raised
from the dead, and is seated at the right hand of the Father? *I do.*

Do you believe in the Holy Spirit, the holy Catholic
Church, the communion of saints, the resurrection
of the body, and life everlasting? *I do.*

When Jesus is baptized, the voice of the Father is heard: *"This
is my beloved son, in whom I am well pleased."* (LUKE 3:22)
Let me ask you a question: do you believe that the Father

---

Easter Vigil or the anniversary of his Baptism renew the promises
of Baptism according to the rite legitimately approved. A partial
indulgence is accorded to the faithful who renew the promises of
Baptism with such a rite [Manual of Indulgences 1999]. The conditions for obtaining the indulgence are: receiving the sacraments
of Reconciliation and the Eucharist and praying for the intentions
of the Holy Father.

addresses this sentence solely to His son Jesus, or to us as well? What do you think? Of course, he is speaking to us too! He is sad to see that many feel too sinful to turn to Him, too unworthy and too wounded. Lots of them do not love their lives and never come to believe that God loves them. Even if they understand it intellectually, they don't reach the point of welcoming this love in to their hearts.

So, in this decade, let's try to welcome the healing that the Father offers us: let's seize upon it as never before! Let's repeat one more time these words: "You are my beloved Son." Now, let's really believe that the Father is speaking about me when He says: "This is my beloved Son, my beloved daughter; in you I find my joy."

It is significant that the Greek word Fragus (ripping, tearing) is only used twice in the entire Bible. The first is used to describe the heavens being opened (Matt. 3:16) when the Holy Spirit descended upon Jesus after His Baptism, and the other time is when the veil of the temple was torn from top to bottom. In these two cases, it's a matter of a supernatural tearing, inexplicable, which echoes the cry of the prophet Isaiah: "Ah, if only you would rip open the heavens and come down!" (Is. 64:1) In this tearing down, God makes it clear that we can enter barefoot into the sanctuary of His heart, into the Holy of Holies, formerly forbidden, to live His life. Let's not forget that the veil of the Temple was at least 10 centimeters thick and between 25 and 30 meters high (according to Joseph Flavius, a historian in this era).

Right now, I'm going to let these words penetrate me, like a balm over my entire being. I'm going to let this word of life soothe me, and heal, little by little, the deep wound that has tormented me for so long: that feeling of being forgotten, abandoned, alone, without a true friend and without emotional security. I'm going to let the words of my Father in Heaven flow over me, the words of my Creator, who has been looking at me through the eyes of His Son Jesus, the Dearly Beloved, since the day of my Baptism: "You are my beloved son, my beloved daughter, and in you I find my joy!"

# The Wedding at Cana

I**T'S ALWAYS FUN TO** go to a wedding: the joy is contagious! Unfortunately, at this wedding feast, the wine ran out. Jesus is among the guests with His disciples, and His mother is there as well. Mary is an attentive mother, who knows how to show her love and see to the needs of each person, a true family woman. She's the first to perceive a problem, but she doesn't worry, because Jesus is there, and she knows that He always has a solution. She approaches Him and says the famous words: *"They have no wine."* Surprised, Jesus answers her with a question, which has been badly translated: *"Woman, what does your concern have with me?"* (JN. 2:4)

To fully understand the meaning of those words, we have to know the Hebrew expression. It's very simple: Ma lì làkh?, which, strictly speaking, means "what's between you and me?" At that moment, Jesus seems to be saying to her: are you aware of the relationship we have, you and I, of my role and your role? Are you aware of the greatness that unites us?

When Jesus calls His mother Woman, it is not to disdain her but to evoke the role of Eve at the moment of creation, a role specifically entrusted to the woman, the spouse of the man, of being a helpmate for him. It is more than a simple assistant, because the Hebrew word for "helpmate" is very rich: it is Ezerah (GEN 2: 18, 20) Here, Jesus defines Mary as the New Eve, who helps the New Adam in His work of Redemption. Jesus is, nevertheless, surprised by His mother's question, because He feels she is pushing Him towards His passion. Basically, from this moment on, Our Lady begins to fulfill her role as co-redemptrix, the one who will collaborate with THE Redeemer par excellence.

When He hears the word "wine," Jesus is shaken to the depths of His inmost being, as He thinks immediately of the word "blood," since He knows three years later, during the Last Supper, He will change the wine into His blood. Afterwards, on the cross, His Blood will be transformed into the Fire of the Holy Spirit, so that He can descend upon His disciples. You see the link? Wine, then blood, then Fire! His mother is there to aid Him in His mission.

Jesus knows that a wedding without wine would be shameful for this family. A lack of wine symbolizes a lack of joy. They are wiped out. In His heart, Jesus undoubtedly says: I, Who have taken the weight of their sins on Myself, Who is here to save the world and bring it back to the Father, I have to act now! A miracle is not enough: I want to change their mortal sadness into joy, my own joy that lasts. That is why I have to endure the cross . . . I can't simply wave a magic wand to save the world."

Jesus is already contemplating the necessity of His passion. The salvation of the world won't come to pass through a simple miracle. If today, in a state of grace, I feel joy in my heart, it is ultimately because Jesus has poured out His blood; every gift from God is impregnated with the blood of Christ.

At Cana, Mary brings to her Son's mind the importance of His passion. With the conscience of a Savior, Jesus anticipates His hour, and so declares: "Woman, my hour has not yet come." These words are of infinite grandeur. Mary understands the message; she realizes what she has stirred up and does not dwell on it. She has confidence in her son's compassion for this couple in difficulty and goes to speak with the stewards. *"Do all that he tells you."* (JN 2:5) She knows that her request will be fulfilled. She is familiar with the promises of Jesus concerning those who pray with faith: *"That is why I tell you: All that you ask for in prayer, believe that you have received it, and it will be given to you."* (MK 11:24)

But let's return to the scene where we find Mary, the stewards and Jesus. Everyone has a role to play and they act accordingly. Mary intercedes. Jesus plays His divine role by changing the water into wine. But what is asked of the stewards, that is to say, all of us? Jesus tells me to "fill all these jars with water." But what connection is there: the lack of wine and the water in the jars? The act of filling the jars does not necessarily guarantee that everyone will be able to drink wine! The joy of the nuptials will not come back because of the water. Jesus pushes me to make a senseless gesture by filling the jars with water, what is the point?

Moreover, by custom it's the women who draw the water at the well, not the men! Jesus has it all wrong, it seems. But Mary knows; she tells me: "Do all that He tells you." Now, filling six 100 liter jars was exhausting work that had to be done in record time. The stewards didn't want to do things by half. They could have said to themselves: "Fine, we'll do enough to please Him; we'll fill one or two jars." No, they obeyed Jesus' order completely! They put all their good will into doing the job. That's the beauty of our relationship with Jesus: He needs us to act. At Cana He needed water as the first ingredient in making wine. But let's go back to our stewards . . . What did they do? They obeyed Jesus without grumbling and without understanding the reason for His demand.

Here's the point to retain: Jesus needs all of our good will to accomplish His miracles. Certainly, if He had had only one or two jars of water to transform, there would have been less wine. Now, water is insipid, without odor or flavor. This is what we can give to Jesus: our troubles, our ineptitude, our weakness, our emptiness and our incapability of reaching true joy. Let us know for certain that when someone gives his ineptness and his weaknesses to Jesus, especially in the sacrament of Reconciliation, He accomplishes that same miracle at Cana, by allowing His grace to flow beyond our human limits. He transforms our nature and makes us capable of what was impossible for us previously: to love, to forgive, to stop destroying ourselves or doing evil.

Look around you: in how many households, once the enthusiasm and the effervescence of natural attraction passes, does the joy diminish little by little to the point of disappearing? That's because we have the water of our natural, limited human condition, which in itself, can neither endure nor produce anything divine. It takes a divine grace to transform it.

Human love has an expiry date, like fresh milk! Let's give Jesus our human nature, let's give Him our lack of joy, our marital difficulties, our existence, which, like water is a little insipid, without odor or flavor.

Jesus cannot act if I don't give Him the first ingredient to work with: without our good will, He cannot intervene in a divine way in our lives. I often recall the beautiful words of

Father Slavko Barbaric, a Franciscan Priest, who was fascinated by Mary's plan for Medjugorje, which he described as mysterious: "There is a grand design for Medjugorje, but we don't know it. As far as I'm concerned, I know that I ought to do all that I can today!" And there you have it: he knows that we must give to God the little we have, and let Him do the rest!

While we pray this decade, let's offer to the Lord the little we have, the little that we are, the little good will that we have, and let Him perform the miracle; He will change our water into delicious wine and make our depleted joy divine. Jesus will replace my poor human joy with His divine joy: "I have told you these things, so that My joy will be in you, and your joy may be made perfect." (JN 15:11). Let's take advantage of it! Let's take advantage of this mystery of the wedding at Cana to ask the Lord to revive the nuptial grace which lives in us.

May those who are married put their wedding rings in the palms of their hands and consecrate anew their marriages to the Lord, by giving to Him all that has become tarnished, so that Jesus can let His wine flow over us, His divine joy. May those who are not married pour out their hearts before Him, because each of us is made for marriage. Our whole being is created to espouse Christ. Many people suffer in their emotional relationships, because they believe that the greatest joy on earth is that which comes from reciprocal love. That secret need buried in the depths of our beings is the sign that we have been sealed with God's love. He alone can truly espouse our souls and satisfy them fully for eternity!

# The Proclamation of the Kingdom God and the Invitation to Conversion

HIS TIME, WE'RE GOING to walk behind Jesus, with Mary His mother. We will see Him accomplish many miracles among the people: curing the sick, dispelling evil and unclean spirits . . . We will see a strength emerge from Him, an extraordinary power! We will hear Him say to the paralytic: *"My friend, your sins are forgiven."* (LK 5:20) Jesus truly announces the Kingdom of God and repeats: *"Repent!"* That is, renounce your maliciousness, let go of your sins, abandon the evil which inhabits your lives and choose the way of light and holiness, and believe in the Gospel. We should rejoice at this news! As we pray this decade, let's decide to respond to the invitation of Jesus, Who talks to us as His companions.

When Jesus sends His apostles to preach in His stead, or even along with Him, He urges them to begin with two very strong exhortations: "Repent and believe!" Contrition for our sins leads us to conversion; it is repentance which predisposes the soul to this change of direction towards God. Today, there are many who fear the word conversion, because they think about the effort needed, the commitment required, and the vexation to be dealt with. So, naturally, they are afraid and hesitate to decide for conversion. The Hebrew etymology of this word, which is still used in current Hebrew, is teshuva, which means return. Yes, but return where? Return to the home of my roots, my Father's house!

Let's take again the parable of the prodigal son: the younger son had his entire inheritance given to him and hastened to depart for far-off lands, because he wanted to achieve a great dream, which in truth was a great illusion. He thought he could find a beautiful and independent life away from home; he didn't expect to fail and return empty-handed!

When he arrived in a distant region, he progressively squandered everything and found himself in a tragic situation where he was abused and left penniless. Basically, he was reduced to caring for pigs (shameful for a Jew! The pork was not kosher!) He couldn't even eat his fill! But it was truly then, in his distress, at the bottom of the pit that he began to think about his return home. A return dictated by hunger, but nevertheless a return. He thought: *"How many laborers under my father have bread in abundance, and here I am dying of hunger!"* (LK 15:17) So, he returned to his home. That was the beginning of his conversion! At his lowest point, he changed direction and returned to the country where he was born: there, where he found abundance, love, and harmony of hearts; there, where he was wanted and had everything he needed to live happily. We understand very well that this house of the father represents the house of our heavenly Father, Paradise.

We also sometimes lose ourselves along the pathways of

sin. During this decade, let's decide to change direction, to return to the One Who loves us unconditionally! Back to this same Father Whom Jesus evokes in the parable of the Prodigal Son. Saint Thérèse of the Child Jesus gives us a beautiful example of how to return to God. Little Therese certainly didn't commit any mortal sins however she was a sinner like us. In her biography, she recalls that one day, realizing that she had sinned, she experienced a great joy! While reading that passage, I said to myself: "Something is not right with her! She commits a sin and she experiences joy? How is that possible?" After continuing the reading, I understood . . . As soon as she became aware of having sinned, she remembered these words of Jesus: *"There will be more joy in Heaven among the angels of God over one sinner who repents than over ninety-nine righteous who have no need of conversion!"* (LK. 15:7) In that precise moment, continues St. Thérèse, "I realized that I was this sinner! So, I threw myself immediately into the arms of Jesus! That done, I ignited great joy in Heaven, and I myself participated in that joy." Wonderful! The moment she perceived her own sin, she fell right away into the arms of Jesus, receiving in return the same joy that God experiences when a sinner returns to Him. This enlightenment is exactly in line with the parable of the Prodigal Son.

And what about us? How long do we wait before throwing ourselves into the merciful arms of Jesus after we have sinned? How long do we flounder in our own muddy hole of self-pity, contemplating our misery, while mumbling: "Well, I knew for sure that I was going to fall into that same sin again! I will never make it! What good is it to keep trying? I'm a mess!" How sad! We are mired in discouragement, or worse, in despair, without realizing that we are providing great joy to Satan! We must never contemplate our misery; that gives in to Satan and destroys our peace! On the contrary, contemplating Jesus turns us unexpectedly and humbly towards His merciful heart and restores peace and joy to the soul!

The return of the Prodigal Son is dictated by hunger. He doesn't say a single word of thanks to his father. He's hungry and knows that in the paternal home, he will find bread. In contrast, his father, full of love, continues to go out to the road, searching the horizon every day, without giving up hope of seeing his son again. The earnest desire of the father is touching: he does not resign himself to living without his son. He wants to find him again and proclaim his love. Let's remember God's cry in the Garden of Eden after the fall of Adam: "Adam, where are you?" He couldn't stand to be apart from his son!

The day of his return, on the last stage of his journey, the prodigal son repeated the confession that he had prepared when he took care of the pigs: *"I will get up, go to my father, and say to him: Father, I have sinned against Heaven and against you. I am no longer worthy of being called your son. Treat me like one of your servants."* (LK 15:18-19) But the father interrupted him! He even prevented him from finishing his confession. He drew him against his heart and expressed his infinite tenderness! He quickly gave precise orders to his servants: *"Fetch quickly the best robe and put it on him; and put a ring on his finger and sandals on his feet. Bring me the fattened calf and kill it. Let's have a feast and celebrate."* (LK 15: 22-24)

For our penance, let us resume our place in the feast of the heart of God. God is so happy about the return of one of His children that He celebrates every time: He's not stingy when it comes to celebrating! That is the good news of Christ; don't look elsewhere for it! Our sins make us sad and miserable: *"Because the wages of sin is death"* (ROM 6:23). We feel terrible with sin. Without knowing it we inject ourselves with a dose of "death," more or less sinister, which will provoke in us oppression, depression, aggressive behavior, anger . . . and, if we don't confess it, it starts to fester and become worse! Sin stagnates in the depths of the heart, works on us, and eats away at us inside. If I want to come back to my Father, I hurry to confess, certain that He is ready to pardon me; or even better, certain that he has pardoned me in advance!

Let's get rid of the ugliness of sin by throwing it into the raging inferno of Christ's heart, where everything burns, where everything disappears. But beware of memories! The Evil One can use them in a very subtle way to tempt us. He is always ready to focus on our sins, by saying, "Do you remember that you did this, that you did that, you fell into a trap? Look yourself in the eye; you always commit the same sin. You really don't believe that you can be a saint, do you? Don't make me laugh!" In this way he discourages us, he cuts us off from that way out, reproaches us for our wickedness, in order to depress us and make us withdraw into ourselves. What did little Thérèse do? She kept her eyes on Jesus, and, in an instant, she went beyond the negative consequences of her sin to the joy of Heaven. She didn't give away one minute to sadness; she didn't withdraw into herself but immediately fixed her eyes on her Savior. That's sanctity! A saint is not a person who never sins. It is someone who doesn't fixate on himself, who does not hesitate for a single instant to take refuge in the heart of Jesus in order to jettison a sin he just committed.

Such is the invitation of Jesus: convert, and come back!

When He says to the paralytic: *"My Son, your sins are forgiven,"* (MK 2:5) He means, participate in the feast of My heart! Jesus came in order to initiate this feast, this banquet of the New Covenant, to which we are all invited. Jesus gave his apostles the power to pardon sins: what joy when we go to see a priest and to hear in confession: "I absolve you from all your sins, in the name of the Father, the Son, and the Holy Spirit." At that moment, the priest acts in persona Christi, that is, through him, it is Christ Himself Who pardons our sins. That's the grace of the sacrament: there is a tangible sign, a voice, a pardon pronounced that we know to be from Jesus. Jesus said to His apostles: *"Receive the Holy* Spirit; whose sins you shall forgive, they are forgiven; and whose sins you shall retain, they are retained." (JN 20:23) He has given this extraordinary power to His priests.

For this decade, I'd like to invite you to search your memory and find the last sin you committed that made you feel sad, and throw it into the burning heart of Christ! Then, let us truly experience our return by saying: "Lord, I'm sad because of this sin, which I never should have committed; but I don't want this evil, I renounce it, and I give it to You, so that You will destroy it. I contemplate Your heart full of mercy, as Saint Thérèse did, and I am running to celebrate with You! I can feel the beating of Your Shepherd's heart, the heart of a Redeemer, Who welcomes me with indescribable joy! I see the Father Who is waiting for me; I return filled with the joy of the Kingdom, and I am making the most of it. I have forgotten all my sins, and I am plunging completely into this celebratory mood. You have given me a ring for my finger, sandals for my feet, a tunic to wear, and you ordered the servants to prepare a fattened calf. I am taking part in the celebration with a free heart; I'm entering into the dance".

# The Transfiguration

HIS MYSTERY LEADS US up a mountain, probably Mount Tabor. The climb is rough, but the view is spectacular. It overlooks all of Galilee, the land of the people of whom it is said: *"Galilee of the Nations: the people who walked in darkness have seen a great light . . ."* (MT 4:16 AND IS 9:1) Jesus climbs the mountain with three of His disciples, Peter, James, and John, and He is transfigured before them.

The mystery of the transfiguration is one of Light par excellence. Jesus unveils all His divinity which was previously hidden from the eyes of His disciples. Jesus wanted to tear down the veil of His flesh, so that they could see not only His glorious body after His terrible and imminent death, but also the glory of their own immortal bodies. The liturgy proclaims: *"Heaven and Earth are full of Your glory!"* and again, *"Tabor and Hermon sing for joy at your name!"* (PS 89:11-12). In effect, all of Creation overflows with the glory of God! The trees, the hills, the plains, the mountains, the valleys, the sky, the stars, the planets, the animals, and all who live in Heaven and on Earth; all Creation is resplendent with the glory of God and yearn for the revelation of the Son of God. "It's an indescribable light," affirms the visionary, Vicka, who was led into Heaven by the Blessed Mother in 1981: "I can find no words to describe the light of Heaven; it's a light which doesn't exist on Earth!"

We too have the potential of being transfigured, of allowing the divine light to enter us. We are temples of the living God, and the Holy Trinity lives inside us. That's why we have to collect ourselves, that is, gather all our faculties, our intelligence, our attention, our memory, our capacity to love, and our sensibility, to contemplate interiorly the One who lives in us. This is the spiritual experience of St. Teresa of Avila: once we enter the nuptial chamber, if we remain in the presence of the Holy Trinity which lives in us, we will become full of light and capable of radiating it.

Among those who have experienced a strong union with God, some have become a sign of the transfiguration for others, like the great Russian saint, Seraphim of Sarov back in the nineteenth century. When young Motovilov asked him who the Holy Spirit was, he didn't answer the boy, but instead transfigured himself before him, allowing a dazzling light to emanate from his face. His face was nothing but light. That young man was overtaken by a profound joy; he felt a great peace, a gentle warmth (in the middle of the snowy desert of Sarov), and he soon understood that the Holy Spirit was manifesting itself to him. St. Seraphim had prayed and fasted for many years. From the time he entered the monastery, he had not stopped looking for that intimate and profound contact with Christ. At sixty-six, he left the desert of Sarov, where he lived as a hermit to re-enter the monastery, in order to welcome and guide the crowds who were coming to see him, because he conferred on each of them his extraordinary gifts.

The more our union with Christ is complete and hidden

in the depths of the tabernacle of our hearts, the more we transform ourselves in Him, and become transfigured. Sometimes the Lord manifests visible signs of transfiguration. For example, the Lord gave a sign to the Sisters of St. Thérèse the Little Flower at the moment of her death at the convent of Lisieux. A photo shows her on her deathbed, radiant! Her face shows no trace of the suffering she experienced: she was illuminated with light. In addition, Padre Pio was so united to Christ, that sometimes people near him saw him transfigured.

> "And as he prayed, the appearance of his face changed, and his clothes became a radiant white ... and there came a voice from the clouds that said, "This is my beloved Son: listen to Him!" (Lk 9:29-35)

Let's do a simple test: let's contemplate right now that light in our hearts, and let's try to look for Jesus as much as possible beyond the veil of our flesh.

Through the lens of faith, let's contemplate Heaven in this divine light and try to make it our absolute priority. I'm insisting on this because there are too many distractions, attractions and preoccupations which distance us from what really counts. In Medjugorje, Mary tells us, "Dear Children, don't forget that the goal of your life is Heaven! Your life on earth is only a brief little stroll compared to Eternity!" Without hesitation, let's take possession of Heaven! This is not a vague promise that the Lord makes to us, namely to "suffer on earth and I will guarantee you Heaven." In fact, it's not about that at all! Jesus has prepared for us a place in Heaven near Him. This place is ready for us, but we must not lose it! It is by conquering death that the Lord has gained Heaven for us!

Our task as Christians is not only to get to Heaven, our final destiny, but to experience Heaven in our hearts right now! All the saints, including those who went through difficult trials, like the venerable French mystic Marthe Robin, have always experienced the joy of the Kingdom in the middle of tribulations, rough times, and storms. These saints wouldn't trade places for anything in the world, because the joy of their loving union with Christ is indescribable! That's what's important and prophetic today: anticipating the joy of Heaven by experiencing that time of grace, which Our Lady talks to us about. The transfiguration is in reality the antechamber of Paradise.

Mary left us another beautiful message: "Dear children, if you abandon yourself to me during your life, you will not even feel the passage from this life to the other life. You will be able to live the life of Heaven already on earth." (Message to the prayer group, August 8, 1986.) If we want a beautiful death, let's live a beautiful life. If I say to you that "Heaven is my goal; it's there that I want to go," it's obvious that I'm not talking about Purgatory. We are obliged to remain interiorly clean, but the will of God is that we are holy and pure, because we have already been purified! Purgatory exists for those who have missed this connection and who did not know how to love enough.

In the same way that there are rules for the road, there are rules for going to Heaven. As you might expect, love should be the center of our lives. The best route to choose is that of love! The Blessed Mother says: "Let love predominate in you, Dear Children! Not human love, but divine love." If I want to go to Heaven, I have to choose the path of love, by giving of myself to the point of sacrifice.

Since we are on Mount Tabor, I propose that we contemplate the splendor and glory of God during this decade. It is impossible to describe such glory. It reflects a union between love and light. In contemplating the glory of Christ, let's set sail anew for Heaven. Certainly, if I pass through gales and tempests and stormy winds, my rudder will be off course and I will quickly lose my sense of direction. Heaven will no longer be my destination. I may then find myself back on the road which attracts me the most and forget that my true destination is Heaven! During this decade, I'm going to put my compass back in focus and aim towards Heaven. If someone or something slows down my pace or, worse yet, puts on the brake, I'll straight away work on getting rid of the problem and, as St. Paul says, finish the race to Heaven.

Now, I will close my eyes and contemplate the marvelous vision of Jesus transfigured. The voice of the Father resonates in my heart: *"This is my beloved Son, the Elect, listen to Him!"* (LK 9:35) I will listen to Him! And what will Jesus say to me? *"Come with me! Follow me! Didn't I pray on your behalf before My Passion?"* *"Father, I will that where I am, those you have given me may also be. . ."* (JN 17:24) I want to go to Heaven with Him. He has prepared me a place by shedding His blood. Therefore I will follow Him at any cost. I will permit Him to live in me and to make my heart His tiny tabernacle!

# The Institution of the Holy Eucharist

IKE LITTLE CHILDREN, LET'S gather in the Upper Room: it's a room upstairs, prepared carefully by Peter and John at the request of Jesus, so that He and the Apostles could celebrate the Jewish Passover; in other words, a room for the Last Supper. We're coming to the table with the apostles, and we're waiting to see what happens, happy to take part in an event so solemn and intimate. I often think of Sister Faustina, who found herself at the Last Supper, and who writes about it in her Diary: "It was a Holy Hour. Thursday. During this hour of prayer, Jesus allowed me to enter the Upper Room, the Cenacle, and I witnessed what happened there. I was most deeply moved when Jesus, just before the Consecration, lifted His eyes towards Heaven and began a mysterious dialogue with His Father. Only in Eternity will we truly understand that moment. His eyes were like two flames. His face, white as snow, was radiant. His entire body was infused with majesty, and His soul full of yearning. At the moment of Consecration, the fullness of love was complete. The sacrifice was fully accomplished. Now, only the ritual of external death, the destruction of the exterior body, needed to be realized: the essence had happened during the Last Supper. I had never yet, in my entire life, had such a profound comprehension of that mystery as I did during that hour of adoration. Oh, how ardently I wish that the entire world could know this unfathomable mystery!" (PAR. 684)

Let's imagine the Last Supper: seated at the table with Jesus, we watch Him take the bread and say: "Take this all of you and eat it; this is My body given up for you." And, at the end of the meal, we see Him take the wine and say: "Take this all of you and drink from it; this is My blood, the blood of the new and everlasting covenant, poured out for you and for many for the forgiveness of sins." Jesus didn't choose this food by accident, the food in which He gives Himself to the Apostles and remains in His Church until the end of the world.

When we eat, the nutrients enter our bodies, nourish all our cells, and penetrate to every corner of our whole organism and regenerate it. The food, in a real way, transforms itself into us. The opposite happens with the Eucharist: Jesus makes Himself food in order to penetrate more intimately into us and to transform us into Himself from the inside. How great is this mystery! It is no longer we who, taking food, transform it into ourselves, but it is Jesus, who, having become food, transforms us into Himself. He enters into the tiniest recesses of our beings, of our hearts, of our souls, of our minds, of our bodies, of our psyches, of our emotions, of our sensibilities, to the point of uniting our subconscious with the other deepest parts of our existence. What could be more beautiful for us, creatures of God? A God Who makes Himself nourishment in order to transform us into Him? It is so good to receive the body of Jesus! In fact it's indispensable! We are feeble people, sinners, so often sick physically and spiritually, and Jesus comes inside us with all His living power.

Marthe Robin said, during an ecstasy: "Oh, Jesus, I thank you, because You take us as we are, and offer us to the Father as You are!"

Another extraordinary characteristic of the Eucharist is that Jesus gives Himself to us in His totality, carrying along with Him every gift, grace, and benediction each soul needs. He transforms us from the inside. He gives Himself in direct correlation to how open our hearts are, and this opening must be free, because He never forces anyone. Jesus truly wishes to give Himself entirely to us. The saints did nothing more than welcome Him in every way just as He was. Often, we retain only a small part of Jesus. We stammer out, distractedly, a prayer like "Lord, thank You for having come," and we don't go any further. We begin to think about something else, and the dialogue is interrupted until the following Sunday.

Now, Jesus' great joy, as He has often revealed to the mystics, is to give Himself entirely to their souls and to communicate His graces. He's not waiting for us to be perfect to give Himself to us; He doesn't give Himself because we are good, but rather to help us become good and to transform us into Himself! The soul which opens itself completely to Jesus permits Him to live in it in all His fullness. That soul allows Jesus to transform it profoundly, immediately. An anecdote from Sister Faustina enlightens us on this point: "Today, when I received Holy Communion, I noticed in the chalice a living, vibrant host, which was given to me by the priest. When I returned to my place, I asked the Lord, 'Why is one of the hosts so full of life, since You are present in the same way under all the species?' The Lord answered, 'That's correct. Under all the species I am the same, but all souls do not receive Me with a faith as vibrant as yours, My Daughter, and that's why I cannot act in their souls as I do in yours.'" (DIARY PAR. 1407)

In Medjugorje, Our Lady has always recommended that we live out the Mass with our hearts: "May the Holy Mass be life for you!" (APRIL 25, 1988) "If you knew, Dear Children, the gifts and graces you received during the Holy Mass, you would go every day, and you would prepare at least an hour in advance!"(Given to Vicka). Jesus is so humble! It's so easy to make Him happy by welcoming Him inside us! When Jesus is inside us with the totality of His person, that's the holiest moment! "That's the most sacred moment of your life!" the Blessed Mother confided to Vicka.

It is during that moment that the Lord dispenses to us all His graces of healing, of liberation, of light, and of peace. It is in that moment of very intimate exchange that He gives us His perfect joy. The stronger this intimacy, the greater and more profound His gift. His sanctity sanctifies us; His strength strengthens us; His beauty beautifies us; His tenderness moves us; His joy makes us joyful: His life makes us live more fully. He gives us His peace, the peace that the world is unable to give. At that moment, the presence of Jesus in us is so concrete that, if we met His mother in the street after Mass, she would fall to her knees in front of us, because she would see Jesus in us.

Jesus doesn't give Himself in the same way to all souls at Holy Communion; some receive Him well, but others receive Him while living in grave sin. With regard to those souls, Jesus said to St. Faustina: "I enter some hearts as though I were going through another Passion."(DIARY PAR. 1598) Before going to communion, it is important to purify our souls with sincere prayer, an examination of conscience, and, if necessary, a good confession.

"Renounce the sin that lives in you," Mary tells us. We sometimes believe we cannot receive Jesus, because we are not worthy. In that case, let's remember the words of Jesus: *"It is not the healthy who need a physician, but those who are sick."* (LK 5:31) We are, therefore, on the list! Jesus likes to work, as He has said Himself: *"My Father works even until now and I work.* (JN 5:17) Even when we open our hearts to Jesus with all our good will, simplicity, and joy, Jesus still finds sicknesses, weaknesses, and bad thoughts. But what joy to have some work to do! Allow the physician of our souls, our Savior, to act. He loves us enough to transform us by His grace! What sadness He experiences when our souls refuse Him, when He sees them so sick and empty! Let's go back to what Jesus told Sister Faustina: "Oh, how painful it is that souls unite so little with Me during Holy Communion. I long for souls, but they are indifferent towards Me. I love them so tenderly and so sincerely, and they don't trust Me. I want to fill them with graces—they don't want to accept them. They treat Me as though I'm dead, but I have a heart full of love and mercy. To help you understand a little of the pain I experience, imagine the most tender of mothers who loves her children a great deal, but the children scorn the love of their mother. Consider her pain; no one can console her." (DIARY PAR. 1447)

When Jesus finds a soul closed to Him in Holy Communion, He doesn't force open the door; He leaves the soul and departs with all the gifts and graces He had so lovingly prepared for it. But His heart is torn with pain! Imagine preparing a fabulous birthday meal for a person you cherish enormously. Everything is ready—the gifts, the flowers, the table . . . but the person calls and says, "I'm not coming!" Imagine how heartbroken you would be! The gifts won't even be opened! How do we treat Jesus, Who offers Himself to us in the Eucharist? Do we feel an emptiness, a lack of love and tenderness? Who could sustain us better than Jesus? Who would rejoice in doing it, if not He? We can't imagine the immense joy He experiences when we open wide our hearts to Him and allow Him to come into them!

In Medjugorje, Mary teaches us to focus on the Eucharist. The center of interest in Medjugorje is not her daily apparition but the Holy Mass! "Dear Children, if receiving my Son in the Eucharist is at the center of your life, have no fear. You can do anything. I am with you." (JUNE 2, 2012) Mary is always beside her Son, always with us as we adore Him, with us as we receive Him! Am I the only participant at Mass? Am I alone before the tabernacle of my parish? I am never truly alone, because the Queen of Peace is with me, happy with my presence. Besides, the entire Heavenly Church is with her: the Angels, the Archangels, the Saints. Isn't that awesome? How many graces we lose if we neglect going to daily Mass when the circumstances permit! The Venerable Marthe Robin used to say: "Our degree of glory in Heaven will be proportionate to the quality of our Holy Communions on earth."

What about the graces we receive during our times of adoration? Jesus is present in the host as a living person, in all phases of His life. We have in front of us the tiny Jesus who is buried in the heart of Mary, the New-born of Bethlehem adored by the shepherds! We have the Child Jesus Who departed in haste for Egypt then lived, hidden, in Nazareth. We have the adult Jesus, a carpenter Who worked with His father, Joseph, and Who delivered work to his customers. We have the Rabbi Jesus, Who taught the crowds during His public life; then Jesus the Martyr on the cross, who died, resurrected and ascended to Glory sitting at the right hand of the Father. We can contemplate Him during all the events of His life, according to our choice and inclination, and meditate on whatever the Holy Spirit is suggesting to us at that moment. The life of Jesus which we contemplate is, therefore, infused and transmitted to us invisibly.

One day, I asked the visionary Vicka what Mary had said to them about Holy Communion at the beginning of the apparitions. Here is the message she transmitted to me: "Dear Children, when you receive Jesus in Holy Communion and you go back to your seat, don't look at other people, nor judge the priest; Dear Children, kneel for at least ten minutes and talk to my son Jesus, who is in your heart." And to provoke her a little, I asked her, "Vicka, are you really sure she said ten minutes?" "No, Sister Emmanuel! She didn't say ten minutes, she said at least ten minutes, a minimum of ten minutes, but, in reality, she would prefer twenty minutes." Basically, it takes twenty minutes for the host to dissolve completely, and these twenty minutes are infinitely precious!

"Go to Mass every day, if the circumstances permit," the Queen of Peace advises us vigorously. How can we waste such a chance to transform ourselves, sanctify ourselves, and improve ourselves? We should always put the Mass at the center of our lives: "Let the Mass illuminate the rest of your day," Our Heavenly Mother reminds us!

One point to remember: when a person has begun his prayer of thanksgiving after Communion, you should never distract him, because at that moment something divine is happening. Why interrupt the secret dialog between the divine host and a soul? Why speak aloud? And to say what? "Did you see the hat of the woman in front of you?" "What are you doing tonight?" Be careful, Jesus doesn't like idle talk!

Jesus said to Sister Faustina: "Write to religious souls that I love to take refuge in their hearts during Holy Communion!" (DIARY PAR 1683) That union is so intense and deep that there is almost a complete identification of the soul with the Lord. When leaving the church, if we run into non-believers, pagans who do not know Jesus, look at them the way Jesus would. Maybe for some of them, this will be the only time in their lives that they will touch Jesus, by touching us! Marthe Robin affirms, "Each Christian life is a Mass, and each soul is a host!" May our entire lives become a celebration of the union of our souls with Jesus!

Sister Faustina understood it well: "Oh, merciful Jesus, with what desire You hastened to the Last Supper to consecrate the hosts I'll receive in my life! You desire, Oh Jesus, to live in my heart and to let Your living blood unite with my own. Who could possibly understand this compact union? My heart encompasses the Almighty, the Infinite. Oh, Jesus, give me Your divine life! May Your pure, noble blood pulsate fiercely in my heart! I give you my whole being. Change me into Yourself, and make me capable of accomplishing, above all, Your holy will and of loving You, oh my sweet Spouse!" (DIARY PAR 832)

I'm going to tell you a story which took place when Sister Briege McKenna was preaching at a retreat for priests with Father Kevin, who often accompanied her. They were at a restaurant and blessed their meal by saying: "Lord, bless our food and those who surround us; come, sit at our table and share this meal with us!" They had barely finished speaking, when Sr Briege suddenly became immobilized, her eyes staring into space. Father Kevin guessed that she was having a vision. As soon as she had recovered her senses, she asked Father Kevin: "Did you see what I saw? Well, when we prayed and invited the Lord to our table, I saw Him come to us, and He spoke to me. There are no words to describe His beauty." She was overwhelmed and trembling. She continued: "He told me this: 'When I am loved, venerated, and invited, I always come!'"

I don't have to tell you that, since then, at our house, Jesus is invited to every meal! Our conversations are never the same. So, why not invite Him more often, even several times per day? If, one day, we don't end up going to Mass, not out of laziness but because circumstances prevent us, we can always make a spiritual Holy Communion, or communion of desire. For that, it is sufficient to invite Jesus into our hearts, and He will be very happy to come to us invisibly. We can multiply our spiritual Holy Communions, hour after hour, by inviting Jesus to spend the whole day with us.

During this decade, I propose that you make a powerful spiritual Holy Communion. Explain to Jesus your desire to receive Him in the presence of Mary, His Mother, and invite Him into your heart. He will come! "Act in me, O Jesus; fix whatever is broken; fill whatever is empty; tend my wounds; heal my illnesses; chase away all the demons which obsess and torment me. Make Your light shine in my darkness; glorify Yourself in me! Be with me in all my suffering; touch me in the deepest part of my heart. Fill me with Your life, Lord. I thirst for You! Come quench me! O Lord Jesus, You are the most beautiful of the children of men!"

# The Sorrowful Mysteries

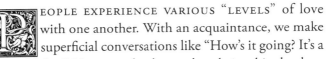EOPLE EXPERIENCE VARIOUS "LEVELS" of love with one another. With an acquaintance, we make superficial conversations like "How's it going? It's a beautiful day!" However, the deeper the relationship develops, the more we begin to care for the person and gradually open our heart to him/her. With someone we love the most, we trust them enough to share with them our suffering, pain and our innermost wounds.

It's the same with Jesus! He wants to draw us into His heart and establish a profound and intimate relationship with us, so that we share in His suffering. The more we love Jesus, the more we participate in His suffering, and the more we want to be with Him at every moment. We start to love Jesus when we desire to share His sorrow and console Him. This is true love, the love which offers itself and which gives itself; it is completely contrary to the egotistical self-centered love which we see so often in the world.

Contemplating Jesus in His passion is, then, the quickest and most effective way to resemble Him. It's good to remember that we become what we contemplate. By contemplating Jesus in the act of extreme love during His passion, we absorb that love: Jesus penetrates us in a divine way, inundating us with His gifts and embellishing our souls. Jesus Himself said as much to a number of saints, notably to Sister Faustina: "My Daughter, your compassion for Me brings me relief. Your soul takes on an exceptional beauty when meditating on My passion. (DIARY PAR. 1657). And also: "It is when you meditate on my sorrowful passion that you please Me the most. Join your small sufferings to all My pain, and they will take on infinite value before My Majesty." (DIARY PAR. 1512)

The closer we come to the suffering Jesus, the more we are vested with His glory. Saint Paul explains this clearly in his letters. We can meditate on numerous mysteries, but it is in the sorrowful mysteries that we truly penetrate into the depths of Christ's heart. We are nourished by His splendor and His glory.

# The Agony in the Garden

S IN THE PRECEDING mysteries, I invite you to close the eyes of your body and open the eyes of your soul, in order to find yourself, in spirit, in Jerusalem. We left Jesus in the Upper Room, where He instituted the Holy Eucharist. When He broke the Bread of Life, He offered Himself entirely, and His sacrifice was already accomplished; only His physical death was still to be realized.

Let's walk with Him and listen to Him sing the songs of the festival with His disciples (MK 14:26). Let's not leave Him alone; let's follow Him into this dark night.

We've arrived at the Garden of Olives. I'm still looking for Jesus with the eyes of my soul. There He is! On his knees, overcome with anguish. He gets up and joins the three apostles who came with Him, His faithful friends, Peter, James, and John, to whom He said: *"My* soul is sad, even unto death. Wait here and watch with Me."* (MT. 26:38) This invitation to keep Him company, He addresses to us as well! He rarely says: "Come with Me!" But at this moment, Jesus has a greater need than ever for our presence and support. We want to stay with Him. We always want to stay with a dear friend, not only when all is going well and life is smiling at us, but always, especially when Jesus or our brothers are in agony.

In the Garden of Olives, Jesus is alone and abandoned, afflicted to the extreme. His sweat turns into blood! What is causing this anguish which torments Him so much? At that hour, Satan is showing Him all the sins of the world, from the first day that man sinned to the end of time. Jesus sees each one of our sins, one after another. At this moment, He is taking upon Himself the sinfulness of all of humanity. His soul is going beyond the limits of space and time, because in the divine light, it examines and intensely feels the repercussions of the lives of all mankind, and of each person in particular: our refusals, our disdain, our indifference, our harshness, our sarcasm, our impurities of every kind, lies, horrors, and the most abominable acts. He sees His Eucharistic body assaulted, with sacrileges and Black Masses; He sees the ease with which people dishonor the extraordinary gift of the Eucharist.

Satan is here, because evil is tenacious. When Jesus is abandoned by His friends and seems overcome by the horror of our sins, the devil tries to crush Him. He does everything possible to discourage him from continuing on His way. What temptation could be worse than showing Him how useless His sacrifice is for so many souls: "You can see that everything you are prepared to do is perfectly useless; men do nothing but sin and they will continue to do so; Your mission is already a failure . . ." And Jesus is able, indeed, to contemplate how useless His sacrifice is for certain souls; He knows already that some will refuse His mercy, even in those last moments granted to the soul for reconciliation with God. The mystic, Marthe Robin, who experienced the Passion of Christ every week for fifty years, said of Jesus that, during His Passion, "a little more and He would have been annihilated".

But Jesus had a secret fire in His heart. From the moment of His conception, His sole desire was to accomplish the will of the Father. Even now at the hour of this supreme trial, we hear Him say: *"Father, if thou art willing, remove this cup from Me; yet not my will but Thine be done."* (LK 22:42) From childhood, He knew quite well that He had come to accomplish the will of the Father. But what is that will? God wants every man to be saved and to open himself up to His immense love, for all eternity. The heart of Jesus burns with that same desire to save us. His love is more powerful than the anguish that torments Him. His love is as strong as the death that awaits Him. He is ready, because throughout His life, He has never failed to accomplish the will of the Father.

We are with Jesus, but, at the time of this agony, we are frightened . . . Fear takes hold of our spirits. We are so afraid that we abandon everything. We fear that the Lord will ask too much of us, that He is handing us an impossible cup to drink! Our humanity refuses it; it cannot even imagine it! And our response is: NO! But what does Jesus say? *"Father, not my will but Thy* will be done." Because of this prayer, the Father conveys new strength to Him!

If we don't say YES like Jesus did, we won't have the strength to do God's will. Following Jesus means abandoning our fears and placing our trust in the Father, even if the cup seems too bitter. The only way out is to humbly renounce and offer up all our fears. It's our humanity that is afraid! What do we do, then, with all those fears we can't shake? That cling to our skin? The fear of suffering too much, to live in agony, to be forgotten, to lose everything or to die.

I invite you to give all those fears to Our Lady and to place yourself in the center of God's will. When we have to undergo a trial or endure suffering, we are seized with such fear that we don't understand anything and can become paralyzed. Or worse, we let God go by the wayside and try to handle our salvation ourselves. No! That's returning to square one! Instead of letting go of God's hand, we should grasp it tighter than ever.

During this decade which we are praying together, let's take Mary's hand again and give to her our greatest fear. She will know how to set it on fire in the heart of Jesus! Who better than Our Lady to free us from the fear of God's will? Is there anyone who can say that he's never known fear? The devil lies to us and wants us to believe that doing the will of God means facing innumerable misfortunes, anxieties, sicknesses, trials, tears, and catastrophes of every kind. He whispers to us, that, on the contrary, getting into the spirit of the world and doing our own will is the way to assure ourselves of happiness and freedom. What a deceitful lie! What fruit do we harvest when we follow our own will and the deceptive attractions of the world? A few flashes of light which spin us around and swallow us up into an ever-growing emptiness! On the other hand, have you ever encountered someone who regrets becoming a saint by accomplishing God's dream for him and adhering to His will? Certainly, doing His will can be challenging at the beginning but surely it is worth the fruits of peace and profound joy which flow from it!

A great source of help is to kneel at the feet of Jesus and consecrate to Him both the moment of our death and the way in which we will die. In that way, our departure from this world will belong to Him in advance. It will happen in peace and without anguish.

Jesus revealed to Sister Faustina:

> "My Daughter, make a resolution never to lean on men. You will do great things, if you abandon yourself entirely to My will, and if you say: 'Not as I will it, but according to Your will, oh God, may it be done.' Know that these words, spoken from the depth of the heart, lift up the soul, in an instant, to the summit of sanctity." (Diary Par. 1487)

These words of Jesus are unbelievable! The summit of sanctity in an instant? Isn't that what I want? Why does it seem so easy? When our Father in heaven hears us speak these words with profound sincerity, He sees His own Son in us! He recognizes the spirit of Jesus! That's the key: to identify with the Son! At that moment, we espouse intimately the Spirit of Jesus; we are one with Him. Without even being aware of it, we are achieving something far greater than constructing hospitals or basilicas! "Father, here I am; I'm ready for anything. Not my will but Yours be done."

Jesus made another promise to Sister Faustina and to other saints who kept watch with him, including those who persevered in Eucharistic adoration, those who continued in personal prayer, and those who remained with Him in their trials. These are men and women who truly sought, from the depths of their hearts, to remain united to Jesus. Jesus tells them, the way He tells Sister Faustina: "Know, My Daughter, that your ardent love and the compassion you have for Me were a consolation to Me in the Garden of Olives." (DIARY PAR. 1664)

How is it possible to console Jesus in Gethsemane two thousand years later? The Agony of Jesus is over! How can a prayer of today help Jesus in His Passion? It's easy to understand if you know that the grace of God has no limits of time or space. What I do today with all my heart consoles Jesus on His way to Calvary and especially in His agony at Gethsemane. So, by watching and praying, we can offer the Lord an immense treasure! What comfort He can receive, then, when the vision of all the sins of the world is overwhelming Him! We don't have to enumerate them, because, today, we are often, sadly, in direct contact with the horror of sin! We see how much man can sin: it's horrendous and terrifying! Those pure and immaculate eyes, which have never communicated anything but love, see terrible crimes and ignominious acts. At Gethsemane, Jesus was seized by a vision of horror which shook him to the core that He actually sweat blood!

I asked a doctor once about whether we can sweat blood, and he responded: "It's impossible for a man to sweat blood, unless he experiences a horrendous shock!"

Still today, we can console Jesus in His agony. It's enough to keep watch with Him demonstrating our will to be with Him and join Him in His suffering and in the suffering of others.

Let's pray this decade while closing our eyes, to see Jesus more clearly! Let's contemplate His divine face, red with blood and bathed in tears. Let's give all our fears to Mary. In doing this, we will not only remain in His company, but we will become one with Him: a single Spirit, a single prayer. "Father, not my will but thy will be done!" The most beautiful prayer in the world!

# The Scourging at the Pillar

N THE SECOND SORROWFUL mystery, we enter with Jesus into the Court of the Roman Governor. We hear the sentence pronounced by Pilate who chooses, against his conscience, to free a murderer and to condemn Jesus to death, death on the cross.

It begins, however, by having Him scourged, a torture reserved for the worst criminals. Jesus knows exactly what awaits Him; He is ready! The law allows a limited number of blows to be inflicted during a scourging, so that the condemned person doesn't die; however, Jesus' torturers, in their demonic violence, lost count. A human body should never have undergone such an ordeal, especially after the Agony in the Garden. It was too much! Saint Bridget of Sweden fervently wanted to know the number of blows inflicted on Jesus during His Passion, and the Lord revealed to her that He received 5,480 lashes from the whip.

He should have perished from this avalanche of blows, but He had to accomplish His great work of redemption. He couldn't allow Himself to die. If He managed to survive the scourging, it's because, once more, He called upon the Father for the strength to endure it.

I find myself near Jesus and I contemplate His divine body, all covered with blood and open wounds . . . Not a single centimeter of His skin has been spared!

Once again, I become the child who began this journey hand in hand with the Blessed Mother. I look at her. She is present for all of it! Every blow resounds inside her, and her heart is torn apart. She knows that legions of angels are ready to intervene, to liberate her Son from this turmoil. Alongside her, I contemplate Jesus, now a living wound, and I am overwhelmed, because His face portrays no hatred. Not a single trace of bitterness, anger, or frustration. In His expression, veiled by blood, I see love and forgiveness, the beauty of a heart which loves despite the ordeal He went through. How does Jesus manage to remain in such love?

Jesus is focused on an immense desire, which prevails over everything else in Him: to save us at any cost! He wants us to be with Him forever! He's not prepared to let us go! His love for us sustains Him, and in the midst of this horror, He holds onto this beautiful dream of making us happy for all eternity.

When I receive a single little blow (whether it be verbal or physical), I admit that my first reaction is neither love nor mercy, but rather anger, frustration and the desire to retaliate! I need time to accept that I need to forgive. While contemplating Jesus I desire to learn from Him how to be merciful.

When we are wounded by a painful event, we become vulnerable. The enemy, so happy to take advantage of our weakness, quickly approaches our wound with the goal of infecting it and making it unbearable. He is an expert in infecting wounds. He has in his pocket so many viruses and poisons at his disposal to infect us! But how does he inject them into our wounds? Think about all the negative thoughts that pass through our minds when we suffer. This is Satan suggesting to our conscience his own thoughts and feelings.

For example, he tempts us with thoughts of despair. "Look. You've already suffered in your life; this time, it's too much! Enough! Put an end to your life! Today, suicide is no big deal. You'll see. In a few minutes your suffering will be over." Satan inoculates us with feelings of hatred and vengeance. "Have you seen all the bad things this person has done to you? It's so unfair! You ought to hate him, him and his whole family; you ought to destroy his reputation! Make him really suffer the way you have. He deserves it!" Maybe Satan will approach us with doubts or with feelings of rebellion against God. "Who is this God who sent you this tribulation? Did you think that God was good and merciful? Forget it! Look at the state He put you in! Do you think that with all the thousands of people who inhabit the earth, He's interested in you? Don't be so naïve! He won't do anything for you! Don't waste your time on Sundays! Mass is useless! Live your life without Him: you'll feel much better!" I could continue with more examples of mental poison because Satan is relentless.

Who hasn't perceived in himself that perverse, tenacious voice which can become an obsession and take over your life? Let's be prudent. Satan is clever and knows very well our particular points of weakness; he knows precisely how to use these weak points to infect our wounds and make them intolerable.

How can we discern that it is he — our mortal enemy — who is tempting us? Easy! In Scripture, we find the Spirit of Jesus at work, in His words and actions. We should ask ourselves the question: would Jesus suggest that I put an end to my life? Certainly not. He came for life! Would He tell me to hate my enemy? On the contrary, He commands me to forgive my enemy and even to love him!

So, there's only one thing to do in these cases of temptation: and that is to radically disconnect! We should throw ourselves into the arms of Jesus, saying, "Jesus, You can see that the enemy is here to tempt me! But all these thoughts are his thoughts; I don't want anything to do with them! They're not mine; I refuse them and reject them! I choose to listen to Your Spirit, Jesus!" So, we fight the good fight which is vital for our soul. It's not easy, but very fruitful.

If we follow the perverse suggestions and directives of the enemy, what do we gain? We will suffer much more and we will lose the little peace we have. Instead, for every subtle temptation of the enemy, let's gather in prayer and ask ourselves: "Would Jesus say that to me?"

Thankfully when a wound inflicts us Jesus also approaches us! He never abandons us. At this moment, He is closer to us than ever and is extremely concerned about our wound! But His speech is totally different, just the opposite of Satan's. Jesus comes to us, because He loves us and suffers with us. Satan feels only hatred for us and wants to tear us away from God; let's never forget that!

Jesus speaks to us in a way far different from the voice of Satan. He speaks with respect, tenderness and humility. He has a profound respect for our freedom, yet we can hardly hear Him. His voice is like a murmur in the depths of our soul, and this divine murmur is only perceived in prayer with the heart and attentive recollection. What would Jesus say to us? "My child, do not be afraid! It is I. I am with you. Look at My hands, My feet and My side. I, too, have suffered. Do not be afraid of anything. You and I together will make it! Just abandon yourself entirely to Me!"

Once Jesus sees that we are ready to abandon ourselves to Him, He asks of us a favor: "Give Me your wound; offer your suffering to Me. Give it to Me!" And if, from the depths of our heart, we give Him our wound, He will not only accept it, but He will see it as a very precious gift. Then, from that moment on, it becomes His suffering. He makes it His own suffering because we give it to Him. Now it belongs to Him. But what will He do with it? Why does He demand it from me? He will place my wound upon His own wound, that of His pierced Heart, so that my wound and His wound make but one reality, one single wound. That way my poor wound, miserable and human, becomes divine, since it belongs to Jesus from that moment on.

All that belongs to Jesus is divine. My injury has become His injury, one single wound united with His! So, with His creative power, He transforms it and transfigures it! Now, what is it that emanates from the wound in Jesus' heart? Bitterness? Hatred? Despair? Rebellion? Certainly not! That divine wound transmits to us His greatest treasures: light, love, compassion, consolation, healing, peace, joy, freedom together with all the sacraments and all the graces of our salvation.

It's important to understand how to make the right choice when we are hit by a trial: Shall I listen to the voice of the enemy who wants to destroy me, or shall I disconnect from him, pray and listen to the voice of my dear Lord who wants to save me? In the first case, I will become miserable and cause my family to become miserable. In the second case, I will receive consolation and joy, and I will help Jesus in His divine work of salvation. Maybe even the salvation of my own family members?! All of us have been given this freedom to choose, so it takes some determination . . .

If I place my wounds in the pierced heart of Jesus, then I participate in the surge of love which gushes forth from that heart and which saves the world. I become, at that moment, a co-redeemer. Instead of becoming intolerable to others and to myself because of my suffering, I become an angel of love and peace. It's not my peace that I give, but the peace of God, which spreads through my transfigured wounds, human wounds which have become divine.

Jesus knows that His wounds are the source of strength for reaching the Kingdom of Heaven. The prophet Isaiah foresaw this when he wrote: *"By His wounds we are healed."* (IS. 53:5) If we place our wounds in His, we help Jesus, and we extend His work of salvation for many more souls. Little Thérèse of the Child Jesus understood it all too well. From her childhood, each time she had physical or inner suffering, she used to say to Jesus: "Take it, my Jesus! It's for You! It's a secret gift for You!" And what did Jesus do? Did He say disdainfully, "What Is that? What sort of rubbish are you giving me?" No, quite the opposite! He grabbed that proffered wound right away and transformed it into a glorious wound by uniting it to His own suffering.

It is my weakness and my misery which draws the compassionate gaze of Jesus upon me, because He alone can transform it into roads to salvation. When He says: "I thirst!" it is evident that He is completely dehydrated, but there is a deeper meaning. He has an overwhelming thirst to transform our wounds into grace and peace.

By assuming our wounds, the divine power of Jesus can operate fully in the world. Saint Thérèse, the Little Flower as we call her, knew well that by giving her troubles and suffering to Jesus (therefore, her wounds!), she became a co-redemptrix. The Blessed Mother also tells us:

> "Today, I invite you to offer your crosses and your sufferings for my intentions. Little Children, give your suffering as a gift to God so that it becomes a beautiful flower of joy! That is why, Little Children, pray for the understanding that suffering can become joy, and the cross a path of joy." (Sept. 25, 1996)

Let's offer to Jesus all our suffering with confidence and love. There is but one Savior, one Redeemer, Jesus, because only His divine blood can redeem us. But, let's not forget that, from Baptism, we all form part of the Mystical Body of Christ and, in that respect, we can help save souls by collaborating with His work of redemption. That's huge!

Through Baptism, we become priests, prophets, and kings. Thanks to the gift of the royal priesthood of the faithful, we have the potential to offer up ourselves and the world to God, becoming in that way co-redeemers. My proffered wounds give a new vigor to the whole human race through Jesus's mystical body, living and real. In Heaven, we will contemplate the splendor of our smallest sacrifices. Offering up my suffering may just help Jesus save a soul doomed to perdition because of his rebellion against God. My offering could enable them to become open and welcome His compassion. It can help Jesus encourage a priest who is in a difficult crisis, help a sick person endure the pain and offer it up, it can help a non-believer find faith, a sinner to repent, a baby to escape abortion, a young one to escape the feeling of despair . . .

"Suffering passes; to have suffered remains," the Little Flower used to say.

It is evident that suffering by itself is evil. It is detestable. The Lord didn't create it. God did not create death either. It's the consequence of sin. But God, from the depths of His immense love, observing how much we suffer, found a way to transform that suffering into the power of salvation for the world: that is the meaning of His cross! The worst sin that man ever committed was to assassinate the Author of life. No one can do worse than that! But by means of the magnitude of His love, God transformed this abominable act into the cause of our salvation. And if He acted in this way for His cross, He will do the same for our crosses. That is why a Christian should not be afraid of suffering, because, through the immense love of Jesus, it becomes an extraordinary source of redemption.

Mary tells us: "Few people have understood the great value of suffering when it is offered to Jesus." (Message shared by Vicka) She also says: "Dear Children, today I invite you in a special way to take the cross into your hands and meditate on Jesus' wounds. Ask Jesus to heal the wounds you have received during your life because of your sins or because of the sins of your parents." (MARCH 25, 1997) Mary affirms that Jesus can heal all kinds of suffering.

At my age, I am probably already covered with wounds, because life is like that, it's a journey full of accidents! But at any particular moment, even at that precise instant when Jesus underwent the scourging, I can unite myself to Him to become someone who transmits His light. My sorrows become a source of healing, of consolation, and of glory!

During this decade, let's close the eyes of our bodies,

open those of our souls, and look at Jesus: His body, His face covered with bruises, but at the same time full of light, love, and glory. What majesty He still radiates! Let's give Him our biggest cross, that hidden wound which afflicts us the most, the one we can't talk to anyone about. Offer it up to Him so that He can be consoled by it: He can then act in us as Savior. My sin will become a beautiful fragrance and my sorrow will turn to joy.

# The Crowning with Thorns

ET'S CONTINUE OUR JOURNEY! We are still in Jerusalem, where Jesus receives the crown of thorns. A number of soldiers are encircling Jesus, and, according to Saint Matthew:

> "They stripped Him and put on Him a scarlet cloak; and plaiting a crown of thorns, they put it on His head and a reed in His right hand; and bending the knee before Him they mocked Him, saying 'Hail, King of the Jews!' And they spat on Him and took the reed and kept striking Him on the head." (Mt. 27:27-30)

We are right next to Jesus and the eyes of our hearts are fixed on Him. Jesus is quiet. Bloodthirsty men surround Him, wound Him, and humiliate Him in every way; they provoke Him, but Jesus remains quiet! I scrutinize Jesus' face, which is covered with blood, mud, and spit, and I can see the splendor of love pouring forth from Him. Jesus remains silent, because, at this moment, He is continuing to perform wonderful work. He is interceding for those who are torturing Him; He is doing good to those who hurt Him. Such is the way of our Jesus!

He can't even see those who are surrounding Him, because His eyes are still drenched in blood. He can barely make out the figures in front of Him, but what does He see? He isn't put off by the monstrous ugliness of these men; He doesn't concentrate on their cruelty or on those faces distorted by violence.

So, what does He see? Beyond the hatred and the scorn, He sees a soul created by God, which is full of great tenderness. "Dear Children, if you saw the tenderness in the innermost part of each person, you would love all men, even the most wicked." (TO JELENA VASILJ FOR THE PRAYER GROUP)

He sees in each soul a formidable potential for love; He sees the reflection of the Father's image, of the Creator, at the bottom of the hearts of these wild beasts! Jesus loves their hearts so much that He thinks only of achieving His great desire: to guide all these sinners to Heaven, to His Father, where they will live for all eternity! He thinks of nothing else, and it is that which gives Him the strength to endure the thorns which pierce His head. He is wearing now that crown of humiliation, which ridicules His real and celestial Kingship.

I contemplate that divine fire which expresses unlimited love and which faces this trial without flinching. I, too, want to love with such ardor! When I contemplate His savaged face, I soak up the love, beauty, and humility of God . . . We become what we contemplate: that's the grandeur of the Rosary!

I am sure of it: when we meditate on the Passion of Jesus with love, all its beauty penetrates us. It's the most effective method of clothing oneself with the splendor of Jesus. He confided to Sister Faustina: "My Daughter, your compassion for Me is consolation. Your soul takes on an exceptional beauty through meditation on my Passion." (DIARY PAR. 1657) And again:

> "One hour of meditation on My sorrowful Passion has greater merit than an entire year of scourging to the point of drawing blood. The contemplation of my sorrowful wounds is of great profit to you and brings Me great joy." (Diary Par. 369)

Jesus continues: "There are few souls who meditate on My Passion with real compassion. I give great graces to souls who meditate devoutly on My Passion." (DIARY PAR. 737)

I, also, desire ardently to enter into His plan of salvation, into the Savior's burning heart! I want to participate in His royal majesty. Jesus is king, not because of the crown of gold that many paintings show, nor because He won the majority of votes. No! He is king because He lay down His life for us out of love: that's the true royalty of Christ!

During my contemplation, I want to let Him transform me, and, when I am there, grieving at His crowning with thorns, I can see that He feels my love and tries to meet my gaze; He wants to communicate His beauty to me. I deeply admire the humility of my king, who allows Himself to be beaten without retaliating; His divine humility gently penetrates me by way of His gaze of meekness. I contemplate His mercy when He intercedes secretly for His torturers. I allow Him to transmit that mercy to me, and it invades me powerfully. From this moment on, I can forgive my enemies, something which is not humanly possible.

Sometimes, we almost feel shameful over the suffering Christ endured. In our countries, even with their Christian roots, people remove the crucifixes from schools, hospitals, and every public place. Are we ashamed of Jesus' suffering? If we chase the Redeemer from the world, we are chasing away our redemption! On the contrary, the suffering Jesus is our pride and joy! Each time our eyes gaze lovingly on Jesus crowned with thorns on the cross, He is profoundly touched, ready to console us, to heal us, to free us from our burdens!

The visionary Vicka recounted to me what took place at Medjugorje on Good Friday of 1982, around a year after the apparitions began:

> "The Blessed Virgin appeared to us with the adult Jesus (she usually appeared with the Child Jesus only at Christmas). But that day, Jesus was suffering His passion. He was wearing the crown of thorns, a red cloak covered with mud and in shreds, the cloak that the soldiers had put on Him to ridicule Him. On His face, swollen and pale, covered with spittle and blood, you could see the tracks of the blows He had endured. It was terrible to see! Then the Gospa said to us: "Today, I came with my Son in His passion, so that you could see how much He loves you and how much He suffered for you.""

I asked Vicka: "Did Jesus tell you anything?" "No," Vicka answered, "He didn't say anything, but I looked at His eyes, and there I saw such tenderness and such love, that it was, for me, stronger than words. I will never forget the face of Jesus!"

Now Jesus is staring me right in the eyes. He knows everything about me. Far from the ugliness and shame of my sin, He sees only a soul to be saved. He is taken with the beauty of my soul. His gaze goes to the depths of my being, and He says to me: "My Child, how beautiful you are! Don't get discouraged because of your sin! I love you, and I see you as you really are. I want to save you; come into my embrace!" So, He re-creates me and transmits to me His divine spirit.

In Medjugorje, the Blessed Mother often tells her prayer group:

> "Right now, go back home and meditate on the sorrowful mysteries of the Rosary in front of the cross! Consecrate your homes to the cross of my Son. If you don't have a priest to do it, do it yourselves. Put the cross on full display in your homes, and say to the Lord: "Lord, here is our house, we consecrate it to Your cross!" You'll see that a plenitude of graces will come down upon you." (To Jelena Vasilj)

During this decade, let's look at Jesus, and allow Him to act deep within our souls. Let Him transform us, fashion us, enrich us! May He make kings of us, so that the love given to us on the day of our baptism reigns with Him in His royal kingdom, where there is neither hatred, nor malice, nor darkness, nor tears! "My kingdom is not of this world," He tells Pilate. The true kingdom of Jesus is found in the Beatitudes: the pure of heart, the meek, the merciful, the peacemakers, and those persecuted for justice. In this moment, under the watchful eye of Jesus, I welcome His kingdom.

# *Jesus Carries the Cross*

ESUS IS NOW WORN out from sheer fatigue. The soldiers brutally load the cross onto His shoulders, with no concern for the open wounds inflicted during His scourging. They jeer cruelly. I am close to Jesus and I contemplate Him while He is scorned by those around Him. He receives His cross as a man welcomes the woman he loves into his long-awaited arms. He bends down to kiss the wood of the cross and prays to His Father in secret. It's unbelievable! Jesus receives the cross as a gift from the Father, a gift He'd been anticipating for thirty three years! He can finally embrace the wood of the cross. He knows that this cross is the instrument of our salvation; that is why He embraces it with such ardor. No complaint escapes from His mouth, only praise. The hour so long awaited has arrived! Jesus stops and murmurs a profound thankyou to His Father for the gift of the cross. Now He can touch it, embrace it, and be nailed upon it.

Saint Frances de Sales, the great bishop of Geneva writes:

"The eternal God, in His wisdom, has always seen the cross He presents to you as a gift from the innermost chamber of His heart. He has looked at this cross He sends you today

with His own eyes, which see everything, and has understood
it with His divine spirit. He weighed it on the scales of His
great justice. He warmed it in His loving arms. He weighed
it with His own hands, to make sure that it wasn't an inch
too large or an ounce too heavy for you. He blessed it with
His holy name. He anointed it with His grace. He perfumed
it with His consolation. And He took one last look at you,
taking stock of your courage. And then, He sent it from
Heaven as a very special greeting for you and a sign of His
merciful affection."

I am that cross for Jesus. Now, I am in His arms, and I can
testify to the love in which He holds me. He feels the weight
of my sins and still carries me lovingly on His shoulders.
Whatever it costs Him, He wants to carry me to the top of
Calvary, so that He can destroy my sins by dying on the cross.
We are intimately united, Jesus and I: we are one!

But Jesus is exhausted; He has lost so much blood! The
weight of the cross is simply torturous and is crushing His
right shoulder. The friction of the wooden beam has made
His flesh disappear, leaving His bone exposed. We cannot
imagine the suffering of Jesus. He can do no more! The soldiers see that. They are afraid that Jesus will die on the way.
That would not be good for them, because they were given
strict orders — the condemned man must absolutely reach
the place of his crucifixion.

They call out to a man passing by, Simon of Cyrene, who
is on his way home from work, and tell him to carry Jesus's
cross. He's a gardener on the outskirts of Jerusalem for the
rich Jewish property owners. After a day of labor, he does
not appreciate having to help a criminal carry his cross! How

humiliating! But he knows that to disobey the Romans is dangerous. The mystics testify that he grabbed the cross violently, full of anger, aggravating Jesus' wounds. But Jesus held nothing against Simon for being rough with Him. He humbly allowed himself to be wounded, but, suddenly, He fell, and Simon lost his footing as well. They found themselves face to face under the cross. So, what did Jesus do then? He fixed His gaze on Simon. No reproach, no bitterness. Jesus opened His heart, and Simon, discovering the face of Jesus in the mud, with bloody tears and everything else that disfigured Him, was stupefied. The last thing he expected in the world was to find such tenderness, such light in this condemned man. He simply couldn't believe it! His soul was upended. In that instant, Simon became a disciple of Jesus, ready to do anything to help Him, to protect Him from the brutality of the soldiers, and even to defend Him at the risk of his own life. Simon carried the cross to Calvary behind Jesus. He would later become a very active disciple in the early church along with his two sons, Alexander and Rufus, mentioned in the gospel of Mark (CF. MK 15:21).

This example teaches us so many things! When the weight of the cross rests heavily on our shoulders, against our will, there remains but one solution: to look at Jesus, fix our sights on Him alone whenever He invites us to carry the cross with Him. At the moment of trial, we must certainly not look at ourselves nor swim in the ocean of our misery! We'll sink! We could fall into a black hole, thinking about our poverty! Looking at our wounds depresses us; contemplating those of Jesus heals us. Focusing on Jesus is the only way to carry the cross without falling over. By contemplating the suffering of Christ, by participating in His Passion, we find strength and grace.

Kathleen, a friend of the visionary Marija in Medjugorje, experienced this. One evening in 1985, she was completely exhausted, because, along with her prayer group, she had spent whole nights on the mountain, and, to make matters worse, she was alone in the house. That night, her spiritual director gave her permission to go to bed early while the others went to Cross Mountain. This permission was a true miracle! There she was at home, alone and happy to be able to sleep finally and to recover from her accumulated fatigue. Her bedroom was on the second floor. She barely had the strength to climb the stairs, each step requiring so much effort. Someone who had fallen into a very difficult situation suddenly came in to her mind. Now, she had promised that woman that she would pray for her that particular night. She let go of that promise and decided she would put off that prayer until the next day. But no sooner had she conquered the last steps on the stairs, she remembered a message the Virgin Mary had given to Marija:

> "When you know that the will of God is that you do something for Him, but that you haven't got the strength, pray to your Heavenly Father that He will re-create you, and He will give you the strength!" (To the prayer group).

Kathleen was chasing away that message. "No, I don't want that strength. My bed is waiting for me!" However, she could feel that Our Lady was asking her to pray. She tried again to resist: "My dear Mother, I want to go to bed. I have permission to go to sleep!" Then, aware that this inner feeling would not leave, she gave in at last to the grace. She got on her knees and called upon the Heavenly Father with all her strength: "Father, I beg You, re-create me now, and give me the strength to pray!" Kathleen recounts that she felt re-generated at that very moment, to the point that she walked up another floor to the chapel, light as a feather, and prayed the whole night long. At dawn, she felt fresh as a daisy, as though she had slept for eight hours. The Father had re-created her. Our mother, Mary, is never wrong!

It's clear that Jesus, also, in His Passion, called upon His Father without ceasing for the strength to get to Calvary, and His prayer was answered! Simon of Cyrene helped Him by taking the cross from His hands and carrying it behind Him. Did Jesus accept Simon's help? Yes. But didn't He declare: *"If anyone wishes to come after Me, let him deny himself, and take up his cross, and follow Me."* (MT. 16:24) Jesus knew very well that for some people it would be impossible to think about taking up the cross: the cross had already destroyed them; they were crushed by suffering, by human cruelty, by alcohol, by drugs, by mental illness. Their strength to do God's will had been reduced to zero. How could anyone ask them to carry their crosses as Jesus did? For these broken ones, it would be impossible! Jesus, in His immense compassion, did not want a single one of His brethren to be ashamed and not succeed in doing what He commanded, so He became weak and put Himself last, so that they would say: "Jesus was with me, He couldn't get there either. Jesus was like me!" When He couldn't carry His cross, He thought about the little ones He loved, the least of the least. He wanted to show them that He Himself did not make it alone. He reserved the last place for Himself!

Very often, Jesus talked about His suffering to His best friends, the mystics, the saints; He said to Sister Faustina:

"You see, those souls who resemble Me in suffering and scorn also will resemble Me in glory; and those who are least like Me in suffering and scorn will be least like Me in glory." (Diary Par. 446)

Jesus also talks to us about forgiveness: "My pupil, have great love for those who cause you suffering. Do good to those who hate you." (DIARY PAR.1628) Sister Faustina answered Him sadly: "Oh, My Master. You see very well that I feel no love for them, and that troubles me." Jesus answered, "It is not always within your power to control your feelings. You will recognize that you have love if, after having experienced annoyance and contradiction, you do not lose your peace but pray for those who have made you suffer and wish them well." And there it is. True forgiveness doesn't reside in emotion, fortunately! The path of life is long.

When we carry the cross, it is good to look at Jesus, who forgave everyone, even us. We have only to open our hearts to receive this forgiveness and give it to others. It's not impossible to carry the cross with love, since Jesus tells us:

"Come to Me, all you who labor and are burdened, and I will give you rest. Take My yoke upon you, and learn from me, for I am meek and humble of heart; and you will find rest for your souls." (Mt. 11:28-30)

There is a huge difference between carrying one's cross all alone and carrying it with Jesus! When carrying it alone, we are quick to become angry or discouraged or annihilated. The Blessed Mother said on 2 March 2018 "Suffering without Jesus leads to despair". On the contrary, if we carry our cross with Jesus, this path becomes a journey of light and even joy. In Medjugorje, Mary tells us: "Dear Children, may your Way of the Cross become a way of joy!" (SEPTEMBER 25, 1996) Jesus alone can transform our cross into joy and even into glory! It's love that brings about this metamorphosis!

During this decade, since we are with Jesus on the via crucis, let's abandon ourselves into His arms; let's allow ourselves to be carried by Him. Let's live there, like a wife in the arms of her spouse. That's what Jesus did by carrying the cross. Jesus confided this secret to Sister Faustina: "My Daughter, today consider My Sorrowful Passion in all its immensity. Consider it as if it had been endured for your sake alone." (DIARY PAR. 1761)

Here I am in Your arms, Jesus! It is not I who carries the cross, it is your cross that carries me. Carry me forever, Jesus! I know that Your happiness is to carry me and save me. Here I am, Jesus! I want to remain in Your embrace!

# *Jesus Dies on the Cross*

ERE WE ARE FACING the most horrible—and at the same time the most beautiful—scene in the history of the world. Horrible because we, the sons of God, have assassinated the Author of Life; the most beautiful because the Author of Life is dying for the Redemption of us all, sinners, and He is washing away our crimes with His own blood. Who do we find at the foot of the cross? Mary, John, Mary Magdalen, Mary the wife of Clopas, the wife of Zebedee, and other women. We, too, want to stay with Jesus during these last hours of agony, and we contemplate Him as He is dying.

According to the Gospel, Jesus speaks seven words while on the cross. We're going to meditate on the ones that are often badly interpreted:

> "From the sixth hour there was darkness over the whole land until the ninth hour. But about the ninth hour, Jesus cried out with a loud voice, saying: Eli, Eli, lama sabachthani?

That is, "My God, my God, why have You forsaken Me?" (MT 27: 45-46)

How can Jesus say: *"My God, why have you forsaken Me?"* We know full well that the Father would never abandon His Son, especially at the moment He was accomplishing completely his will!

God allowed Jesus, during His Passion, to experience a terribly painful and total spiritual night, to the point that He no longer felt the love of His Father, nor His connection to Him as a son. That's the most painful of spiritual nights! *"For our sakes, He made Him to be sin who knew nothing of sin,"* as St. Paul affirms. (2 COR 5:21) And, again: *"He is a propitiation for our sins, not for ours only but also for those of the whole world."* (1 JN 2:2) Jesus experienced the rejection of the Father on our behalf, and, through this atrocious suffering, He reconciled us to our Creator. All the suffering of the Passion culminates in this spiritual night. Jesus sensed the absence of the Father, Who seemed to be ignoring His suffering and rejecting Him, and this evoked in Him a feeling of total failure. He felt rejected because He had taken our sins upon Himself. It was as though what He had endured thus far had served for nothing. Jesus had borne it all, thanks to His connection to the Father. But now that He didn't perceive His presence and felt rejected, everything seemed absurd. All the demons of despair were attacking Him. It's hard to imagine the enormity of His consternation. Why did the Father want this? He wanted it for our salvation. Jesus had to go through this terrible experience of us being cut off from the Father, so that we could find communion with the Father again and access eternal life! He wanted to endure being disconnected from the Father in order to reconnect us to the Father. We are looking at an unfathomable mystery of compassion! How could we find greater love?

Let me explain. When we were in the Garden of Eden, through our own sin, we broke our communion with the Father, our Creator, and lost the state of grace; we fell into darkness. We lost awareness of God, of His friendship, and of the gift of conversing with Him. But God, Who is pure love, wanted to renew this connection and accepted the fact that His only Son would have to sacrifice Himself. In order to restore this connection between us and the Father, and between the Father and us, it was necessary for Jesus to endure an interrupted communion with the Father, to feel abandonment in His divine soul by experiencing indescribable suffering. And it was necessary that He feel truly abandoned. We understand that truth, because He did not cry out, "Father, Father, why have You abandoned Me?" He could no longer say "Father," because it seemed to Him that the Father was no longer there, so He cried: *"My God, my God . . ."* He had reached the point of no longer feeling Himself as the son of God who was sacrificing Himself, but like a sinner, who, having lost God, exclaims his abandonment. Three hours in this state, three interminable hours in this darkness, the darkness of the whole human race in every era, in a heart who had never committed a sin!

After those three hours in darkness, His soul was able to see His Father again. God's plan had been perfectly accomplished, and Jesus cried out: *"Father, into Your hands, I commit my spirit. And having said this, He breathed His last."* (LK 23:46) Because Jesus suffered through that death on the Cross, no one should despair any longer. Jesus drank the heavy cup for us. (CF. IS 51:17-22) He experienced all of our darkness, until the Father came to His rescue, thus restoring the connection of mankind to the Father. He destroyed our despair. Jesus gives us a marvelous strategy here. Whenever we are downhearted to the point of feeling death in our very souls, whenever all seems lost and the devil seems to be prevailing, we can and should cry out to the Father, in an almost inexplicable act of confidence!

Let's look at Mary, the most beautiful example of all creatures. She contemplated her Son enduring unimaginable suffering, giving out His last sigh, and dying. She stood there, at the foot of the Cross. Imagine the inner turmoil of this mother! She, the mother, the woman of perfect compassion, immaculate, with no trace of hardness, the tender mother, who experienced in her body and in all her being the suffering of her Son. During the anguish and the agony, she could have said: "Father, is this really Your plan? You're content to see Your Son in this state?" She could have rebelled against the Father, but she had faith in the midst of every trial, unlimited confidence in the plan of God. Despite everything her innocent eyes saw, she repeated: "God is good; God is love! God is good; God is love!"

In times of darkness, our salvation is to give our hand to Mary and repeat with her: "God is good. I believe it! He's going to transform this darkness into true light. I'm going to be patient a little longer . . ." Let's be sure that the light will come, a light never before seen, the one you see at the end of the tunnel, the most beautiful of lights, the one that brings victory over darkness, over sin, over death, over Satan and all of Hell. It's the true light which lasts forever, which never tricks, nor betrays, nor disappears.

During this decade, let's take Mary's hand and offer our darkness to Heaven. Let's offer that feeling of abandonment, which afflicts us when we no longer see the direction our lives will take, when it seems to us that the end of the tunnel will never arrive and the night will be prolonged indefinitely. Let's resist the demon who takes advantage of our weakness and taunts us, saying: "You see, Heaven doesn't exist! You're living in a dream world. Talk of salvation is a trap. The Resurrection doesn't exist. It's all a lie! You can see very well that you've been abandoned! Why struggle anymore?"

I beg of you, don't listen to that demonic voice! Listen instead to the voice of Mary and the murmuring of her prayer, which keeps saying over and over: "God is good. God is love. God is good. I believe; I believe in love. I believe in the Resurrection!" Let's cast our darkness upon the heart of Mary, and let's wait with her for the hour of the light. We are going to wait for it with her unshakable confidence, with her motherly heart overflowing with tenderness, because, for sure, this light will come.

"Dear Children," Mary tells us, "I am with you, by contemplating and experiencing in my heart the Passion of Jesus. Little Children, open up your hearts and give me all there is inside, the joys, the sorrows, and every single pain, even the smallest, so that I can offer them to Jesus, and, so that with His incommensurable love, He may burn your sorrows and transform them into the joy of His resurrection." (FEBRUARY 25, 1999) When she appeared in Medjugorje, Mary always left a cross behind her. I don't mean a bloody cross, but a cross of light, as a sign of victory! It's the sign that the suffering is at an end and the Resurrection is coming!

# The Glorious Mysteries

HAT A PARADOX! ON the one hand, we believe that our final destination is that of being glorified one day in Heaven; on the other hand, we don't know what the word "glory" means! A mixture of divine love and uncreated light? A mysterious reality inaccessible to our comprehension?

The desire for glory is imprinted on each of us like an indelible seal. But, since the fall of Adam, we seem to have lost contact with the deeper part of our being. The world proposes to us an earthly and very temporary glory: success, power, notoriety, fame, popularity . . . all that is simply vain glory, as St. Paul emphasizes! When Jesus speaks about the lilies of the field, He adds: *"Even Solomon in all his glory was not arrayed like one of these."* (MT. 6:29)

By traveling through the glorious mysteries with Jesus, we try to make this thirst in us for the true glory explode, that true glory that only the Resurrection can obtain for us, the glory that awaits us in Heaven with all its delights and of which we often savor a pre-taste in prayer.

# *Jesus' Resurrection from the Dead*

E ARE IN JERUSALEM: Jesus has died on the cross. It's over. He's already buried. An enormous stone prevents access to the tomb, and soldiers are keeping guard. Tonight, Jerusalem is particularly dark. I, too, am devasted by the events of last Friday. We are all overcome with pain and with a crushing feeling that all is lost. We had so hoped in this exceptional man, this prophet, this Rabbi, who spoke to us as no man had ever spoken, not to mention the signs and wonders He brought about! For us, He really was the long-awaited Messiah, the One who would liberate Israel!

Night has fallen on Israel. The Sabbath is over and I can't sleep! Yes, the holy city is plunged into an oppressing darkness. A heavy silence, made of tears and groaning weighs heavily on the disciples. An insufferable sadness. No one says a word. Peter himself doesn't know what to do; as for the Apostles, they are wandering around without purpose, like lost sheep. Their grief-stricken hearts cry out in the night, and they don't want to be consoled. They have lost everything in losing Jesus. At this point, why live? The thought that this darkness will endure forever crushes them. Total defeat! The beautiful story of Jesus is over.

Only Mary Magdalen, driven by her immense love for Jesus, goes out of her house at dawn, even though the sun has not yet risen. She is accompanied by several women: Joan, Mary the mother of James, and Salome (CF. MK 16:1). Fixated on the tomb, she runs towards it. Even though she is in despair, there remains one small act to accomplish for her Jesus; she is anxious to make an ultimate gesture of love for Him: she wants to anoint His body with the most precious aromatic oils. When she arrives at the tomb there is a huge surprise! How is this possible? The heavy stone has been rolled away! By whom? She searches in vain; the body of Jesus is no longer there! She has not yet understood that she shouldn't be searching among the dead for the One Who is alive. However, she was with the disciples the day when Jesus announced that He would rise on the third day! But the horror of the cross had made her lose her senses.

And suddenly, there was Jesus in front of her! Jesus in person, truly alive! He is risen! Her heart is beating frantically!

There are no words to express the joy of Mary Magdalene and to describe the beauty of the Risen Jesus! Jesus all light! Jesus all tenderness! Jesus all glorious! Jesus more radiant than ever!

I, too, a shy little child, approach timidly . . . I have never before seen Jesus like this! I admire Him in silence, in ecstasy. I adore Him with all my soul . . . has He not conquered death? Have we ever known anyone who left the tomb by Himself? Jesus has not finished surprising me; death has not been able to keep Him in its grasp! On His face, I read the joy of the victory He has just won on our behalf! He set us free! He conquered death; He vanquished my sin. Hell, with all its rebel angels, has been brought down. But, oh, how much this victory has cost Him!

Jesus sees my heart thirsting for love; His intense gaze rests on me and penetrates the depths of my soul, and He welcomes me with love, just as I am. Right now, He wants to fill my heart with His love and His light, and I want to let myself be filled; I crave it! What would my life be like without this victory of light which is being offered to me? Nothing! I want to experience this resurrection, this new divine life that only the resurrected Lord can give me! And He longs to give it to me! His desire is that each soul completely experience this divine life and transform itself to the point of resembling Him: He, the uncreated light, the beauty, the love! I go to Him, then, with no fear, and, as never before, I open my heart to the Risen One with blind trust. Jesus tells me: "Peace be with you! Be filled with My light. I have come to heal you of your inner emptiness, of all sickness, sadness, and lukewarmness." I am opening myself up to you, Jesus, because You alone can quench my thirst for love.

However, there is a woman who didn't need to go to the tomb! Why go to see an empty tomb? Why search among the dead for the One who is alive? Mary, the mother of Jesus, never stopped believing. She knew that after three days her Son would rise again, as He had proclaimed it. She believed so much that she waited for Him in the Upper Room, the place where the disciples had hidden themselves and which had become a place of fear and tears.

Thanks to revelations from the mystics, we know that before even going to find the women at the tomb, Jesus went first to see His mother. He found her in the Upper Room, in prayer, and, while embracing her as a beloved Son, He announced to her His victory over death. He thanked her, because Mary, despite the apparent victory of evil, had never stopped believing.

I too, oh my Mother, want to continue to believe and love, even when there is no one left who believes, when everyone abandons Jesus, and it seems all hope is lost. I will not let evil triumph! You told us, Mary: "Dear Children, through love, turn into good what Satan wants to destroy and appropriate for himself." (JULY 31, 1986)

Here I am, Mother! Like you, when I see evil at work, when I observe its apparent triumph around me, in my family, and in all the circumstances of my life, I want to continue to believe firmly that Jesus is coming to me and that there is a way out. You hoped against all hope. I want to walk hand in hand with you, oh Mary! Teach me how to remain faithful and hopeful in every situation, even the most destabilizing. I am a child of the light and not a child of darkness. I want to integrate into my life your message:

> "Dear Children, I would like you all to be reflections of Jesus and to bear witness to this unfaithful world that walks in darkness. I want you to be a light for all and testify to the light. Dear Children, you are not called to darkness but to light. So, be a light by the way you live your lives." (June 5, 1986) *

Yes, Mary, I want to respond to your call, and today, more than ever, I decide to believe in the Resurrection!

The word "believe" in Hebrew doesn't mean: "I think that

---

* Words from Heaven: Message of Our Lady from Medjugorje, St James Publishing (1 May 2010), Pg. 243

. . .but I'm not really sure." No! Emouna in Hebrew means to adhere to a reality, to adhere to a person. When I say, "I believe that Jesus is risen," I affirm that I am one with Him, and that I adhere to Him as risen.

Dearest Jesus, I thank you for the heavenly light with which You want to fill me. Come, Lord, and remain in me! Forgive my doubts, especially when I think there is no way out of my situation! It is You, Lord Jesus, Who is the solution to all problems! From this day on, I will try to cling to Your victory, to make it my own, and to fill myself with your light. I believe in the resurrection of the dead; I unite myself to Your divine heart, more powerful than all the forces of evil combined. O, Jesus, I believe in Your resurrection!

# The Ascension

E ARE NOW ON the Mount of Olives, the place where Jesus taught the 'Our Father' prayer. The eleven are hanging on His every word as He assigns to them the great mission of spreading the Good News to the ends of the earth. I have again become that little child, and I'm enthusiastic about this task. It's surprising to see how much confidence Jesus has in us! *"Go, therefore,"* He tells us, *"and make disciples of all nations, baptizing them in the name of the Father, and of the Son, and of the Holy Spirit, teaching them to observe all that I have commanded you."* (MT. 28: 19-20) Thank You, Jesus! If we believe that Your words can be made flesh in our lives, then let us be Your voice, Your hands, Your steadfast gaze, Your heart. You call us to accomplish wonders!

I fix my eyes on Jesus: while He ascends towards Heaven, He raises His right hand to bless His apostles. He disappears while blessing them; it's His last gesture on earth, His last visible sign. This blessing is an immense treasure! To truly comprehend its significance, let's consider together the meaning of the word "blessing," which is braha in Hebrew. The correct translation of the word "benir" (to bless, in English) is not "bien dire," (in English, to speak well) as the Latin translation suggests. In reality, the one who blesses takes from the immense treasure of God a little bit of Him and transmits it to the soul of the one receiving the blessing. The blessing of God penetrates directly to the soul to enrich it, without appealing to the senses and the intelligence.

The blessing that Jesus gives to the eleven when He ascends to Heaven is not limited to those who are present at the scene, but reaches all the baptized, including us. Today, we can always take advantage of the grace of the Ascension of Jesus and live fully within His blessing.

However, that grace is not automatic, as the Blessed Mother affirms: "Dear Children, you work much but without God's blessing." (MAY 25, 2001) So, it's crucial to remain within Jesus' blessing! Mary never stops reminding us to put God before everything always: whatever we are doing, let's begin with a prayer and finish with a prayer; that way, we will be certain to have offered everything to God. The goal of our lives is to live for God and to glorify Him in all things; such is His will. If we always act in this way while He watches, we will remain under His blessing, like the fish so happy to dance in the sea which is their natural place. God will be with us and we with Him.

If we are not well-established under the blessing of the Lord, it's because we don't think about Him; we don't live for Him; we live as though we have nothing to do with Him. We don't live for Him when our own will drives all our plans. In these cases, we bypass His blessing, and all we undertake has no value, because we have achieved it without God's blessing. Understanding that is fundamental! If God doesn't occupy the first place in our lives, we can define ourselves as Christians, but we will live and work without His blessing. If we don't live for Him, we live automatically for this world and its earthly values. Some of Jesus' words are commented upon too little in our parishes: *"Every plant that my heavenly Father has not planted will be rooted up"* (MT. 15:13). However, it is never too late, because this divine blessing is always offered to us; Jesus is always anxious to bless us. How sad it is that we don't seize these opportunities for grace, when it is so simple to place ourselves under the shower of God's blessing. It's sufficient just to decide firmly to reserve the first place for Him.

God never stops blessing us, particularly through His priests. At the end of each Mass, the priest gives Jesus' blessing to all the faithful who are present. What is holding us back at that moment? We receive the same treasures and graces that Jesus gave to the Eleven that day! No more, no less. At the end of the Mass, Jesus in person blesses us through the hands and words of the priest. Again, Mary tells us: "Dear Children, don't receive the benediction of the priest in a superficial way, because it is Jesus in person Who is blessing you; be aware of that." (MIRJANA, DECEMBER 2, 2006)

In Medjugorje, our heavenly Mother gives us her maternal blessing, and she specifies: "Dear Children, I am giving you my maternal blessing, but that of the priest is greater than mine, because he receives the anointing of his hands when he is consecrated as a priest." (TO MIRJANA) Clearly, Mary is not a priest. She is the mother of God. Mary adds this message, which has left so many priests dumbstruck: "If priests knew what they were giving when they gave a blessing, they would bless day and night!"

In the gospel of St. Luke, we find a beautiful confirmation of the power of God's blessing: *"They prostrated themselves before Him; then they returned to Jerusalem with great joy."* (LK.

24: 52) How is that possible? A disciple might say: I have lived with Jesus for three years; I have been able to listen to Him, talk with Him, feel His presence, eat and drink with Him; I never left Him. . .then, all at once, He disappeared from my very eyes! I would feel like a widower who had lost the joy of his life and his reason to live. I would have every right to feel overwhelmed with sadness. But the Apostles, on the contrary, leave full of joy! What happened? Through His blessing, Jesus transmitted His divine power and joy, so much so that they are filled with Him!

The blessing is a means which permits Jesus to remain with us every day until the end of the world. His benediction is incredibly powerful! Even if I were to find myself on a desert island in the middle of the ocean with no possibility of encountering Him in the Holy Mass, I could still live under His blessing if I wanted to. This is the way He connects with me. Wherever I am on earth, His hands, which bless me, pour out abundant graces on me! What good news! We know that sadness plunges us into a state of inertia, which prevents us from giving a blessing, while the Eleven *were continually in the temple, praising and blessing God."* (LK. 24:53) They were like fountains, overflowing with praise and joy!

Jesus reunites with the Father, and there, at his right-hand, He becomes our advocate. He shows the Father unceasingly His wounds of light and glory, the marks of His overwhelming love for us sinners. The wounds of Jesus are a constant plea in our favor before the Father. In return, seeing at what price Jesus saved us from sin and death, the Father, Who loves us, unleashes upon us torrents of mercy. Our greatest friend, our divine defender, is there, seated at the right-hand of God, the Father. He didn't come to judge the world but to save it, and, from the highest Heavens, He continues to save the world through His wounds of light.

Lord Jesus, I thank You, because You have not abandoned us. You are always with us, and from Heaven, You never cease to work in our hearts. We thank You for the precious hope that You give us through Your Ascension. You have assured us that You have reserved a place for us: *"In my Father's house, there are many mansions. Were it not so, I would have told you, because I go to prepare a place for you."* (JN. 14:2) Oh, thank You, Lord, for having reserved a place for us! We want to stay there forever with You, because all that we love is in You.

Let us now intercede for all those who do not know You, because, at the bottom of their hearts, they don't know, as we do, the wonderful hope of having a place near You forever! O Lord, today touch the hearts of even those who do not know Your love! Many live in the shadows, in sadness and sometimes despair, overcome by the burden of life and all kinds of trials; yes, all those brothers and sisters who don't have the means or strength to hope! You see how difficult it can be in the world today. In the streets, in homes, in offices, You see that Christian hope has disappeared . . . O Lord, this hand You have raised in blessing — we see it also in the painting of the Merciful Christ that You Yourself gave to Saint Faustina for the whole world; help us also to become that hand extended towards our exhausted brothers, alone in their trials, those who live in insufferable spiritual solitude! You reminded us through Mary:

"Dear Children, anxiety has begun to reign in hearts, and hatred reigns in the world. That is why you who live my messages must be the light and extended hands to this

faithless world, that all may come to know the God of Love."
(November 25, 2001)

Yes, Jesus, help us to become Your extended hands towards
this world which ignores You, to bring Your children under
Your divine benediction, so that they know there is a place
for them with You, in Your heart.

# The Descent of the Holy Spirit

WE ARE NOW IN the Upper Room in the city center of Jerusalem. I am a little child in this upper chamber with Mary, the Apostles, and the disciples to see what is happening. As it is written in the Acts of the Apostles:

> "And when the days of Pentecost were drawing to a close, they were all together in one place. And suddenly there came a sound from heaven, as of a violent wind blowing, and it filled the whole house where they were sitting. And there appeared to them parted tongues as of fire, which settled upon each of them. And they were all filled with the Holy Spirit and began to speak in foreign tongues, even as the Holy Spirit prompted them to speak." (Acts 2:1-4)

This whole event was truly remarkable! Coming from nowhere, flames landed on their heads and they were filled with something never before seen on earth; a fire of love, of light, an explosion of overflowing joy! It was the third person of the Holy Trinity, the Holy Spirit, the union of love between the Father and the Son.

At the heart of the Holy Trinity, among the three Persons

who together are one God, the Holy Spirit personifies the exchange of love between the Father and the Son, a love of communion. That same Spirit is given to us, so that we love God and love one another the way that Jesus loves us. It is He who helps us to love and who rejoices in this same divine love: *"Love one another, as I have loved you,"* (JN 13:34) Jesus tells us. The fire of love which burns in the very center of the Trinity is given to us. What a sublime gift! The Spirit of God brings us gifts of incalculable value, which Saint Paul enumerates in his letter to the Galatians: *"Charity, joy, peace, patience, kindness, goodness, faith, modesty, and continency."* (GAL 5:22) Who wouldn't want to allow the fruits of such a Presence to burn in his heart?

I could expand on this idea and give multiple examples, but I would rather invoke this Spirit. We need Him so much! My dream is to be totally filled by the Spirit which unites the Father to His Son, the Spirit of communion, the flame of love! Our hearts are often too cold, empty, solitary and lost. Let's recollect ourselves now, close our eyes, and free ourselves from every fear. Let us let our vain thoughts drop away and call upon this immense love, this flame of love. Let's pray for it together:

"Come, Holy Spirit, send a ray of Your light down from Heaven; come, Father of the poor; come give us Your gifts; come, Light of our hearts. Supreme comforter, gentle Host of our souls, sweet freshness. In labor, rest; in fever, coolness; in tears, comfort. Oh, Light of happiness, come fill to the fullest the hearts of all your faithful. Without Your divine power, there is nothing in any human which is not perverted. Wash what is dirty, drench what is dry, heal what is wounded.

Loosen what is tense, warm what is cold, make straight what is crooked. To all who have faith and who trust in You, give Your seven sacred gifts, give merit and virtue, give salvation in the end, give eternal joy. Amen!"

In Medjugorje, Our Lady often invites us to pray to receive the Holy Spirit and to welcome His gifts:

"What counts most is to pray to the Holy Spirit, that He will descend upon you; when you have the Holy Spirit, you have everything. Pray for the gift of the Holy Spirit; when the Holy Spirit comes, peace is secure; when the Holy Spirit comes, everything changes around you; the Holy Spirit wants to be present in families; allow the Holy Spirit to enter; He comes through prayer. That is why, Dear Children, you should pray and allow the Holy Spirit to renew you and to renew your family; when the Holy Spirit comes down to earth, everything appears clear and transformed; let yourself be radically guided by the Holy Spirit; your work will go well." (According to several messages given to Jelena Vasilj)

And also, " I am preparing you for the new times that you may be firm in faith and persevering in prayer, so that the Holy Spirit may work through you and renew the face of the earth." (JUNE 25, 2019)

Mary explains that the Holy Spirit is our great friend and that it is sufficient just to call Him, and He will come. Our call to Him is never in vain!

Some time ago, on the day of Pentecost, a woman in Medjugorje invoked the Holy Spirit unceasingly, all day long. She lived every second turning her heart and soul towards the

Holy Spirit. But in the evening, she felt quite disappointed, aware that nothing had happened. She said to herself: "I did not know how to pray to the Holy Spirit, but I never stopped invoking Him!" The next day, a man approached her and said, "I thank you deeply, because last night at dinner your words touched me so much that I felt I had been changed; I received immense grace from the Lord." That woman understood that the Spirit of Wisdom and Love had really come, but she wasn't aware of it. Have confidence, then! When you call upon the Holy Spirit, He hurries to meet you.

The little Arab, St Maryam of Bethlehem, had an extraordinary devotion to the Holy Spirit and had this prayer on her lips at all times: "Holy Spirit, inspire me. Love of God, consume me. Along the right path, guide me. Mary, my Mother, look down upon me. With Jesus, bless me. From all harm, all illusion, all danger, preserve me." What struck her the most was that this grace was offered to every soul: the grace to allow oneself to be inspired by the Holy Spirit.

In Scripture, Jesus said it clearly, *"Ask, and it shall be given to you; seek, and you shall find; knock and it shall be opened."* (LK. 11:9) And again, *"Therefore, if you, evil as you are, know how to give good gifts to your children, how much more will your heavenly Father give the Holy Spirit to those who ask Him!"* (LK. 11:13) How can anyone doubt those words?

On the other hand, let's pay attention and not miss His coming! The example of the saints guard us against a subtle danger: the souls of the religious, as well as pious people who live in the world, have a routine, a schedule in which they allow the Holy Spirit to call them at particular times. These souls would not know how to respond to unexpected inspirations which may occur at any moment; for example, while washing the dishes. They tend to limit the Holy Spirit to a particular time slot, meaning His spontaneous promptings are ignored. If souls are not attentive to the call of Love, they might multiply their NO's, big or small, forming a sort of "antibody" against the Holy Spirit. In that case, they may no longer be able to listen or be led by Him. They are "vaccinated" against the Holy Spirit. This can often happen to a consecrated soul, which is even worse because the religious, the consecrated souls and the priests are the ones who have received this call to beckon the Holy Spirit to earth and so they bear a great responsibility. St Maryam of Bethlehem used to say "Within religious orders, persecutions reign; jealousy rules among the religious orders, and that is why the world is in darkness."

The visionaries of Medjugorje say that a white cloud surrounds the feet of the Blessed Mother. That's the sign of the presence of the Holy Spirit, who will never abandon her. It's the same cloud that accompanied the Hebrews in the desert, as it is written in the book of Exodus:

> "And the Lord went before them to show them the way,
> by day in a pillar of cloud, and by night in a pillar of fire:
> that He might be the guide of their journey at both times."
> (Exo. 13:21)

The Holy Spirit always lives in Mary: she's the most perfect temple for Him. Those who hold her hand live in the presence of the Spirit. Saint Louis-Marie Grignion de Montfort used to say that "when the Holy Spirit finds the love of Mary in a heart, He flies there!" The sign of the presence of the Holy Spirit in a soul is charity, that is, divine love. If the

Holy Spirit lives in us, it is impossible not to be charitable. Saint Paul deals with this characteristic profoundly in his letters, making it clear that the sign of the presence of God is love, not miracles, prophesies, or speaking in tongues. All the gifts are marvelous, but it is only charitable love which shows that we have been anointed. Someone who is open to others, always ready to help and to give of himself entirely, is a person who loves!

St Maryam of Bethlehem received a message from Jesus about the holy spirit which I would like to share with you. He said to her that "Whoever invokes the Holy Spirit, will look for Me and find Me. His conscience will be as delicate as a flower in the field. If the person is the father or mother of a family, peace will reign in his family, and his heart will be in peace in this world and in the next. He will not die in darkness, but in peace." He also addressed His priests and said: "I ardently desire that priests say a Mass each month in honor of the Holy Spirit. Whoever says that Mass or hears it will be honored by the Holy Spirit Himself. He will have light; he will have peace. He will cure the sick. He will awaken those who sleep."

Let's pray this decade by asking this divine love to invade us with all His power, and let's invoke together the Holy Spirit:

- Spirit of love and truth, come into my heart!

- Spirit of wisdom and science, come into my heart!

- Spirit of counsel and fortitude, come into my heart!

- Spirit of mercy and forgiveness, come into my heart!

- Spirit of modesty and innocence, come into my heart!

- Spirit of humility and chastity, come into my heart!

- Spirit of consolation, come into my heart!

- Spirit of grace and prayer, come into my heart!

- Spirit of peace and kindness, come into my heart!

- Spirit of Holiness, come into my heart!

- Spirit which governs the Church, come into my heart!

- Spirit of God Most High, come into my heart!

- Spirit who fills the universe, come into my heart!

- Spirit of the adoption of the sons of God, come into my heart!

# The Assumption of Mary into Heaven

ARY WENT TO HEAVEN in a very distinct manner, as her soul carried her body up with it. We on the other hand are familiar with the body being detached from the soul at the moment we leave this earth. I would like to bring you into this scene, in the same way I have done until now. This time, our destination is no less than Heaven itself! Let's imagine the arrival of the Blessed Mother in Heaven. There she is, standing right there. After some sixty-five years spent on earth, she has finally returned home! You can imagine her saying to Jesus: "Here I am, my Son! You see, I have done your will; I have achieved perfectly the dream of the Heavenly Father for my life!" With what joy and tenderness Jesus takes her into His arms and presses her to His heart! I open my eyes wide and see them together in an indescribable light. It is a unique scene, in which God welcomes the most beautiful of His creatures and gives her the glorious homage she deserves! After having endured so many joys and so many hardships on earth, there they are together forever in the glory of Heaven!

While contemplating Mary in this light of infinite glory,

I feel both pain and an ardent desire to find myself one day in the embrace of Jesus. Pain, because I am not there yet. Joy because that is my destiny; I will present myself one day before my God. Certainly, I will not be able to say like Mary: "O, Jesus, I have accomplished your will in all things!" That would be a terrible lie and a ticket straight to Purgatory. On the contrary, I will have to say to the Spouse of my soul: "Jesus, You know that I am a sinner, but I have tried hard to do your will. I have failed countless times, but day after day, thanks to your mercy and the grace of confession, I have started again, and I have put all my good will into following you." I know that God looks at the heart, while the world takes into consideration only our results and success. What will Jesus say to me? I hope that upon seeing my good will and especially my trust in His Divine Mercy, He will welcome me into His arms. "We obtain from God what we hope from Him," affirms Saint Theresa of the Child Jesus.

Vicka recalled one day this message from Mary: "You know, Vicka, on earth there are people who pick and choose when it comes to God and doing God's will. They take a little bit of Scripture and a little bit of the world. These people have already decided to go to Purgatory." (PRIVATE MESSAGE TO VICKA) With a certain sadness, Ralph Martin, founder of the Charismatic Renewal in the USA, calls them "cafeteria Catholics," because they choose what they are going to take and what they are going to leave. Compromising behavior!

Then Mary continues: "There are people on earth who have consciously decided to do everything they can against God and against His will. These people have already decided to go to Hell, unless they convert." We know that, throughout the world, there are those who have made a pact with Satan to oppose God and His works. They do enormous damage, and, unfortunately, they are multiplying in droves today! A tragic reality!

And Mary adds, finally: "There are people on earth who have decided to please God at any cost! These persons have already decided to go directly to Heaven." Directly to heaven? Is this possible? Yes, of course; our own firm decision is going to put us into one of these three groups. We will have, in the other world, what we have decided to have here below. That's part of the teaching of the Virgin Mary. "Dear Children, may today be the day when you decide for holiness!" (NOVEMBER 25, 1998)

I believe that each one of us would like to go directly to Heaven, right? But we know that it is much simpler to find ourselves in the first group; that is, among those who only take part of the Gospel seriously and ignore the rest. Without even being aware of it, we organize our lives, and sometimes the lives of others, down to the smallest detail, putting aside the will of God. Or, maybe we ignore the acts of Providence: "Yes, I believe that God is my Father, but I have never seen any miracles. Yes, I trust in God, but He doesn't intervene in my life. Praying and confessing frequently is great, but it's too much for me!" But, but, but . . . My friends, take care not to destine yourself for Purgatory! The time spent there is far too long and painful, more painful than the greatest suffering on earth, the mystics tell us!

Let's ponder the moment we arrive in front of our Creator: Jesus will show us a marvelous place that He has prepared for us with great care having paid the price with His blood, and it is there, with immense sadness, that we will become aware that we have accomplished only 50% of His will for us. We will find ourselves saying: "Yes, Jesus, I only loved You to a certain degree. I have to acknowledge that I was occupied with a thousand other things that I considered more important than you. I only realized half of your plans for me." We shall see then the other half, the part we neglected . . . It will be a piercing wound. We can't choose that! Let's choose to accomplish 100% of the plan God made for us! It's really too good to be missed!

Jesus tells us: *"I am going to prepare a place for you."* (JN. 14:3) We might believe that we have the right only to a tiny place, a kind of spare pull down seat in one corner of Heaven, far from the great saints like St. Francis of Assisi, St. Catherine of Siena, the Curé of Ars, Padre Pio of Pietrelcina, St. Theresa of the Child Jesus, St. Faustina, Mother Teresa, and so many other fabulous saints that we know! Would God really be that mean? Has He created a small number of souls of supreme quality who will achieve great spiritual heights, and all the rest of mediocre quality? We all carry the seal of the blood of Christ within us; its value is inestimable. Our souls, as cherished spouses of the Lamb, are protected by it! God has a perfect plan for each of us, and He wants to accomplish it fully for each of His creatures. The Creator has not failed anyone; we are all called to a perfect sainthood, not a discounted sainthood. Such is the dream of God: that the wonderful place He prepared for us in Heaven will not remain empty!

Alas, there are many believers who ignore completely this place reserved for them in Heaven, and, due to a lack of energizing motivation, waste their time on earth with nothingness and lose direction in their lives. Our Mother in Heaven has often reminded us that eternal life exists:

"Dear Children, you have wandered far. You have taken the wrong path. Don't forget that the goal of your life is Heaven! But Satan never sleeps; he diverts you through modernism, materialism, and egoism. You are attached to the earth and all earthly things. After this life, there is all eternity." (May 25, 2010)

Dear friends, throughout this decade, I invite you to choose Heaven! We can 'right this ship' and choose to occupy the place that Christ has obtained for us at so great a price. Let's stick to the plan of God without hesitation, so that He may accomplish His dream for you. And what a dream! That's what Theresa the Little Flower did. From early in her childhood, she was familiar with trials and suffering. She was hypersensitive, very traumatized by the loss of her mother when she was four and then by the successive departures of her two sisters at the convent of Lisieux . . . In short, everything made her suffer, and she cried at the least little thing.

She could have shut herself away to live in sadness and to be depressed for the rest of her days, discouraged and destined for a miserable existence! How did she manage to become a great saint and even the youngest doctor of the Church? What was her secret? What did she do more than us? One day, these words of God resonated in her heart: "Be holy, because I am holy!" She understood that her great weakness could not be an obstacle to the plan of sanctity that God had for her. She would receive the grace to become a saint, because such was the will of God, and God doesn't ask something without making it possible. So, without delay, she made the firm decision to become a saint! Even better: to become a great saint! She believed in the infallible power of God and she decided to welcome the plan of holiness that God had for her life. There you have her secret: she decided! And God did His own part . . . Few people realize that we are all called to great sanctity! It's a matter of occupying fully the best place that Jesus has prepared for us, whatever our present situation is and whatever wounds we carry. Even if I were a great sinner who was very old, it would never be too late to capture that grace! We can become great saints only if decide to be so! Our Lady has often exhorted us:

> "Dear Children, may today be the day that you decide for sainthood. Don't wait until tomorrow! Decide to put God first in your lives!"

You could compare the spiritual life to a sea voyage. I am in a boat on the Mediterranean and want to get to Marseille to join my family. Wanting to attain my goal, I set my course for Marseille, and I point my rudder in the correct direction. In spite of the waves and storms (tests and temptations) which come pelting down on my small boat, I will arrive safe and sound, because I oriented my boat towards Marseille. But if I neglect to watch carefully, if I stretch out on a deck chair to get a tan, while admiring the lovely coastline of the Mediterranean, I become distracted and let my rudder do anything it pleases. Then, I risk drifting at the whim of the waves, and I will not arrive in Marseille.

The Mother of God tells us: "Dear Children, don't forget that your real home is in Heaven!" Let's consider the energy we might use to obtain the retirement home of our dreams, or to acquire a car that will make us proud. But, one day, that will disappear! The car will end up in a scrap yard and our bodies will deteriorate and waste away too! It would be tragic to arrive at the last station of our life and see that we have prepared nothing for our eternal home, the only one that will last forever! Why not care for it with love, starting today?

I take Mary's hand again and orient the rudder of my life towards sanctity, towards my ultimate destination, which is Heaven, where God's embrace is waiting for me.

Many people think that sanctity consists of performing extraordinary deeds and miracles. Certainly not! Even Satan, who is an angel, can perform amazing deeds to deceive us! Others think that sanctity consists in becoming someone exceptional, and they exclude themselves from this group. No, apart from those who have a very specific call from God, the simple and obscure life is the surest way. What, then, is true sanctity? It is, quite simply, having in our hearts the fulness of love. That's why the saints are the happiest people in the world! When we don't have love inside us, we become ill! We can obtain this plenitude of love through prayer, the sacraments, and charity. Through them God fills us with His love, like a constant drip of graces, and, day after day, we grow on the path to holiness.

Many people fear that the will of God will cause them pain, because they have a false idea of it. They see it as both restrictive and negative. They think that it will deprive them of this or that, and, especially, that it will prevent them from freely doing what they want. That is ignorance of the living God! God wants only one thing: to save us at any cost. Jesus declared: *"Even so, it is not the will of your Father in Heaven that a single one of these little ones should perish."* (MT 18:14) What are we asking the Father when we say: "Thy will be done"? We are pleading with Him to save all His children.

We are saying with all our hearts: "Here I am, Lord! I want to collaborate with your plan of salvation for all humanity. Use me any way You wish, because I want to participate fully in Your mission!" The will of God is the very lifeblood of mankind!

In this mystery of the Assumption of Mary, we receive a momentary view of Heaven where we witness the poignant embrace between Jesus and His mother, which prefigures the embrace we will have one day. We admire the victory of love which Mary brought to earth and which merits such happiness for her! Like a true mother, she wants all her children to be near her. She waits impatiently for us to take refuge in her arms, so that we can rise with her, give ourselves to Jesus and reign with Him!

# *The Crowning of Mary as Queen of Heaven*

FOR THIS MYSTERY, WE are again invited to our Celestial Kingdom. I invite you once more to Heaven, this time to see the joy of Jesus, the Father, and the Holy Spirit, when they crown Mary Queen of Heaven and Earth. We can be proud of having such a Queen, overflowing with love and tenderness! She's a Queen and a Mother, a true Mother!

Let me ask you a question: for you, what is a Queen? What is a King? Recall for a moment the fairy tales of your childhood, in which the majority of Kings were, more or less, despots. The history of mankind is replete with so many examples of Kings who abused their power so much so that, for "the people" that we are, the simple words of "King" or "Queen" can stir within us an uncomfortable feeling. All the same, a King is a person who possesses a kingdom, a territory, a country, essentially a place which is, by law, under his dominion. In this kingdom live his subjects, and, in the particular case which occupies our minds, the subjects are each one of us. But it is out of love that we want to submit ourselves to our Queen, Mary! We love her and desire to please her. What part does she play? Like a true Queen, she governs the country by trying to guarantee the peace and well-being of everyone!

We are now on the last mystery of the rosary. We have been the beloved children of Mary for nineteen mysteries; now, we are called to become her subjects as well and to step up a notch in becoming concretely united with her. That reassures us so much! She is Queen because she loves! And because she loves, she is entirely at the service of our happiness. This process of contemplation has made us grow in the knowledge of Jesus and Mary, and we have finally understood that we can, without hesitation, entrust our lives to them. We confirm to them that from now on we welcome them as our sovereigns, we want to consecrate ourselves to them, as well as all our loved ones, and all that belongs to us. Through a beautiful prayer of consecration, we tell Mary that we belong to her completely and with all our heart.

Unfortunately, a moment after pronouncing this prayer, it can happen that we act in the spirit of the world, forgetting to whom we belong. We distance ourselves from her, and we forget that all we are and all we have by rights belongs to her. During this decade, we are going to renew our act of submission to the Blessed Mother, the Queen of our entire lives. The example that follows will help us comprehend quite concretely the extent to which she wants to enter our everyday lives. We're going to let her reign there and guide us to peace and to the capacity to love in words and action.

I'm going to invite the Mother of God to my house, yes, into my home, so that she can see all the rooms. She will know then how I live with my husband, my children, and all my family and how I take care of the house. I take her hand and introduce her first to my bedroom. I ask her:

— Mother, I would love it so much if you were the Queen of my bedroom! Do you like it? How will she answer me?

— Yes, it's a beautiful room! I see that you have changed the curtains. It's so much brighter like that! You even bought a new mattress; that will be better for your back!

A little later, a veil of sadness passes over her face, and I ask her:

— Mother, is there something not right in this room?

— My dear daughter, I don't see my son Jesus here! Where is the crucifix? Where did you put it?

— You're right, Mother, I re-arranged that closet, because my daughter told me to put the poster of that American actor on the wall, and I listened to her. Mother, it's true. I got rid of your Son from the wall!

— My child, you know very well that it is not that American actor who saved you! He's my son, too, and I love him, but please replace him with the Crucifix. Before going to bed, get on your knees in front of Jesus, you and your husband, and pray together. Reconcile yourselves if necessary. Don't go to bed without having made peace. That way you will live and sleep with the blessing of God! You'll see the difference. Also, put some sacred objects in your home; make your home a blessed one. Your life will change, and you will be better protected.

—Okay, Mother! I'm going to put the Crucifix back in its place right now; that way, you will reign over my room with joy!

—Thank you! I see a photo of your late mother-in-law on your dresser. Have you had Masses said for the repose of her soul? Don't neglect that: you can't imagine the graces that you will obtain helping the souls out of Purgatory! You will make new intercessors for yourself in turn, intercessors who will help you in your life here below.

—Now, Mother, let me show you my dining room. Do you like it? I consecrate it to you. Be the Queen of this room!

—I see that you have bought beautiful chairs and that you have a large table. Just as my Son does, I like big tables; it reminds me of the meals at which my Son drew sinners to conversion and where the poor had their places. But, you see, I'm a little sad. Around this table, I've never seen the poor or the suffering of any kind, the blind, the deaf, the sick, the handicapped, the homeless . . .

—O, Mother, I have often read that passage of the Bible; I know it practically by heart, but I acknowledge that I have never thought of putting it into practice! I have never invited people like that. Mother, I'm ashamed. I'm sorry. I've offended your Son! But look! I have an idea: starting today, it is you who will issue the invitations! I will ask whomever you want to invite, and I will try to welcome especially those who cannot give me anything in return, exactly as Jesus said. Rejoice! You're going to be the Queen of my dining room!

— Mother, now let's go see the living room! It's delightful, right? What do you think of it?

— Delightful for you, but not for my Son . . . Why did you put the television right in the center? Don't you remember my message at Medjugorje: "Dear Children, set aside a corner for family prayer." If you want to keep your family together, the very best way is to gather together in prayer every day. If not, the enemy will find no obstacle to his work of destruction, and he will come to sow discord! He will steal the little peace that you have and take pleasure in dividing everyone! Make a little altar, and put on there a Bible, a cross, a little cup of holy water, an icon . . .

— Mother, I've already thought of that, but, you know, I am always so busy . . . You're right, I'm going to move the TV and organize a beautiful prayer corner!

— Mother, look, there's a telephone here, a land-line. I want you to be the Queen of this indispensable instrument. What do you say to that?

— I thank you for thinking of that, because with a telephone you can do as much good as you can evil. If you let me reign over your telephone, I have good news for you: your bills will be cut in half!

— Really? Why?

— Think about it! If I am beside you when you call someone, you won't be able to say bad words or to slander anyone, you'll avoid useless talk and damaging words, you'll no longer say anything bad about your neighbor; bad-mouthing will cease! Imagine how much time and money you will save! What joy this will give me, who suffers so much because of your land-line and cell phones! I will be delighted to inspire in you good conversations for the glory of God. And moreover, do you remember your sick elderly aunt whom no one visits? Why don't you call her once or twice a week? If I am the Queen of your telephone, you will transform it quickly into an instrument of charity! My Son will be happy, because, as He said: "Whatever you do for the least of my people, that you do unto Me."

— Oh, Mother, why didn't I consecrate my home to you earlier? You are truly a Queen. You take care of the tiniest details of our lives!

— Now, I'm anxious to show you the DVD's and the books in our library. Do you want to take a look at them? What do you think of them?

— You have a large collection! A lot of these DVD's and books are good. But I see that some of them contain impure and violent scenes. That saddens me, because that's the way you introduce darkness into the hearts of your children, who are so spiritually sensitive! They ought to discover the beautiful things of creation and marvel at them. Why inoculate them with these poisons? Why connect them with antichristian theories, like those of the New Age and others, so that their gift of discernment diminishes? I propose that you separate them all and put them in two piles: one which are good and you are going to keep; the other with what does harm and should go into the garbage to be destroyed. Please don't even think of giving it to someone and infest that person! Burn all of it! My Son does not like compromise in the homes of those who are baptized and belong to Him.

— Oh, Mother, I said to myself so many times that I should pay more attention, but, you see, I accept compromise so easily! Now that you live here with me, I will have the strength to change.

— Mother, would you take a peek into this safe where we put our valuables? I want you to reign over all my material and financial goods and over all that we possess.

— My dear child, thank you for entrusting your money to me. You manage it well, but I see that you often forget what the Lord advises in Scripture, that is, to tithe to the Temple, which means giving 10% of your income. (CF. LK 11:42) The Temple no longer exists, but the poor are always there. Sometimes you do give a little money to the needy, but you can give even more to them! Do you know what the Bible teaches us about almsgiving? *"For alms deliver from all sin, and from death, and will not suffer the soul to go into darkness."* (TB. 4:11) *"Alms deliver from death and purge from sin."* (TB. 12:9) *"Almsgiving atones for sin."* (SI. 3:30) You'll see just how the Lord will compensate you! So, set aside that tithe; you'll never regret it. Think about those who are in distress today; there are more and more of them! Such as a family which has nothing to eat, a mother hospitalized, a father out of work, a poor person, a young person in need . . . You could do so much good! Jesus will give you back a hundred-fold; He likes to multiply His rewards when someone gives freely, even the smallest thing. You still count your money too much; be generous in your almsgiving!

— Dear Mother, I promise to be more attentive. I already feel a great joy at the idea of helping a number of people. Thank you for recalling for me those words of your Son!

— Mother, I want to show you the closet of clothes in the hallway, okay?

— I see that you have good taste, that's a good thing; but I have one remark to make to you: that dress that you bought the other day, do you remember any thoughts you had in choosing it?

— Yes, Mother, I'm ashamed to admit it . . . I confess that I was immodest! I bought it with the intention of attracting attention, being seductive. By wearing it I might inspire in others impure thoughts and mental sin in some ways. Thank you for bringing that important point into focus! You can see how often I sin without even being aware of it! I don't consider the weakness of people around me and how easily they could fall into sin because of me. Oh, how I repent from this! It's time I give you your place as Queen! I have an idea: from now on, you can go shopping with me and you can tell me what you would choose for me to buy. Since you are the most beautiful woman in the world, I have nothing to fear!

—Mother, come, I want to show you my garage! This is my car! I want to consecrate my car to you so that we can travel the journey of life together.

—My child, I thank you, because I never had a car in Nazareth, and I'm not hiding from you the fact that I love to lead the way. How many times have I said in Medjugorje: "Dear children, I am your Mother and I want to lead you to Heaven!" Thank you for letting me guide your life. My child, you would really let me drive your car?

—Yes, Mother! Take the wheel and drive me wherever you want, or wherever Jesus wants!

—My very dear child, I see that, sometimes you are in anguish thinking about the future: so, you often have the temptation to consult seers, astrologers, fortune tellers, or those who invoke bad spirits by reading tarot cards or stars. Do you know that God calls that an *"abomination"* in the Bible? (DT 18: 12) How many times have you read your horoscope in the newspaper with some curiosity? Stop all that! Know that if I am driving your car, if I am guiding your life and I am by your side always, you have nothing to fear. You cannot know the future now. Live the present moment in profound peace without fear of anything! When night falls and you don't see anything, I see! When you drive at night, your headlights only light up the part of the road you need to go on further; you don't see your entire journey. If you did you would be totally confused, you wouldn't be able to manage all the information, and you would be completely overwhelmed. I really want to make this covenant with you: I will give you all the light you need to go forward in peace, as long as you have unlimited confidence in me. Does that work? After all, am I not your Queen? I thank you very much for having let me enter your house in the intimacy of your life and of having accepted my Queenship. I assure you of my blessing always.

Dear friends, if we make a firm decision to welcome the Blessed Mother as our beloved Queen, she will bless us! We can confide in her and consecrate to her our lives, our dear ones, our homes, our work, and all our earthly possessions, so that she reigns in our homes as the best Queen ever. We will not be disappointed.

Dear Mother, I thank you for truly being my sovereign! With total confidence, I welcome you into my life. We all belong to you, Dear Mother, and we love you infinitely!

# Mysteries of Compassion

OMPASSION ISN'T BORN IN a heart in twenty-four hours! Like clear water, it seeps in slowly and penetrates little by little inspiring a person to behave differently which can lead them a long way. It's a matter of allowing yourself to be taken over by a new pain, that of your neighbor, a pain which makes you suffer but which has within it the gentleness of love. *Cum patior,* "I suffer with," that's the sense of the word compassion, which designates one of the most noble of sentiments of the human heart, a sentiment worthy of the nobility of Christ. This is the opposite of that frosty indifference which degrades mankind. This shared pain, desirable among all others, permits the soul to grow in charity and obtain the greater glory of Heaven.

The Gospels present us with numerous examples of true compassion. Why, then, don't we imitate St. John Paul II, who, in his audacity, wanted to enrich the "classic" rosary with five new mysteries taken from Scripture, the mysteries of Light? Why not choose five episodes from the life of Jesus where you find the fulness of compassion?

There is no mercy without compassion, because compassion is the anti-chamber of mercy. So, in order to step over the portal of Compassion, the only one which gives access to Heaven, let's learn, through Mary, how Jesus manifested His compassion towards the people who surrounded Him; let's fill ourselves with His example! Isn't that the desire of our hearts and the purpose of our lives: to resemble Him in everything and to configure ourselves to Him as much as possible? Of course, because we become what we contemplate . . .

# The Good Samaritan

N THE FIRST MYSTERY of compassion we are on the road leading down from Jerusalem to Jericho. Jesus encounters a Doctor of the Law, who asks him: *"Good Master, what do I have to do to inherit eternal life?"* (LK 10:25-37) Jesus answers him: *"What is written in the Law?"* The Doctor of the Law says in return, *"Love the Lord your God with your whole heart, and with your whole soul, and with all your strength, and with your whole mind, and love your neighbor as yourself."* But the Doctor of the Law, trying to justify himself, insisted, "And *who is my neighbor?"* Jesus gave an unequivocal answer, when recounting this striking parable:

A man was attacked by robbers and left half-dead in a ditch by the side of the road. A priest passed by there but continued on his way. Then a Levite came near the place, but he passed by him also. Finally, a Samaritan — a stranger who was not part of his Jewish community — began to follow the road, and discovering the wounded man, was moved with compassion and went swiftly into action. He stopped to help him. What took place in the heart of this Samaritan? Quite simply, he took upon himself the suffering of that man.

There are many who experience feelings of compassion:

it is difficult to see a sick person, someone who is suffering, without being moved. However, true compassion does not consist only in experiencing an emotion: it moves us to actively alleviate the pain of the one who suffers, as much as possible.

When he discovers this stranger, the Samaritan is so affected by his suffering that he forgets everything else. He approaches him, and, without wasting any time, treats him like he would his own son.

Let's analyze the chronology of his actions, as they are presented to us in Scripture. There are nine of them:

1. He sees the victim and is filled with compassion.
2. He approaches.
3. He tends to his wounds by pouring oil and wine over them.
4. He bandages them.
5. He puts him on his own donkey.
6. He takes him to an inn.
7. He takes care of him.
8. The next day, he takes out two coins and gives them to the innkeeper.
9. He says to the innkeeper, "Take care of him; whatever more you need, I will repay you on my way back."

It's worth our while to focus on this last part. The Samaritan took a huge risk, because the owner of the inn could have taken advantage and presented him with an enormous bill!

The emotion the Holy Spirit inspired in him enflamed his heart so much that he didn't think at all about the consequences of his choice; he took no account of the risks or the disadvantages to himself. He also wasn't deterred by the fact that in helping this man he could catch the same disease. All of this helps us understand that the opposite of compassion is indifference.

Now, the Devil is an expert when it comes to removing from us any trace of compassion and in establishing within us that dreaded indifference. The moment that an inspiration of charity, compassion, or forgiveness is born in our hearts, we are also bombarded with thoughts that neutralize us on the spiritual field of battle: "I don't have time! This is not a good time! It'll cost me too much! Who knows what's going to happen to me if I do that! This person doesn't deserve it! I'm not capable of it! It's too late! It's too early! He's going to take advantage! I don't know anything about this person!" The list of excuses is endless.

This scripture is beautiful, because, while the directive seems demanding, Jesus is giving clear instructions. Basically, He is inviting us all to do what He asks the Doctor of the Law to do: *"Go and do likewise!"* Jesus doesn't say for him to do half or one fourth or three fourths of it, no! He says do the same and you will have eternal life. The trophy is, therefore, eternal life! The more I demonstrate my compassion by addressing the pain of my brother, the more I receive the promised happiness in return, the advanced payments of true life: peace, joy, love . . . and the closer I'll be to Jesus. I will also become a fountain of love for others.

The Doctor of the Law wanted to know who his neighbor was. Jesus' answer is clear: your neighbor doesn't exist! Every man is your brother. But the real neighbor is you, when you draw close to your brother to the point of sharing his suffering and comforting him. When you are the one who is merciful, it is you who become your brother's neighbor.

Let's consider the example of Mother Teresa of Calcutta. She left the convent of the Sisters of Loretto, where she had everything: happiness, nourishment, security, the warmth of a community, and the real possibility of growing in holiness. But, following a singular call from God, she found herself again alone in the populous streets of Calcutta, without the help of anyone, solely because of her love for the poor and those in pain.

Another beautiful example of compassion is given to us by Gianna Beretta Molla. She discovered that she was pregnant, but serious health problems arose during her pregnancy. Because she was a doctor, she knew very well what awaited her: she was going to have to choose between her own life and that of the child she carried. Imagine the dilemma! She already had several children, still young. In spite of that, she didn't hesitate for one second: she chose to save the life of the little creature she was carrying in her womb, who she had never seen.

I think, also, of a great French friend, a wonderful mystic, still not widely known: Mother Yvonne Aimée of Malestroit. During the Second World War, she managed a hospital and experienced great compassion for all the soldiers, who risked being deported to concentration camps. She pitted herself against the Nazis and hid allied soldiers who the Gestapo were looking for, by allowing them to pretend to be hospital patients. She knew that, if she was caught, she would be tortured and killed; but she wasn't thinking of her own life; she was more concerned with the desperate situation of those men in danger of death. She devoted herself to saving them and thought up ingenious plans by concealing them in the habits of hospitalized religious.

Let's think, also, of two great saints, Sister Faustina Kowalska and Padre Pio of Pietrelcina, to whom God gave the gift of reading souls. That's another way to show compassion. When Sister Faustina crossed paths in the hallway with a person in a state of mortal sin, she quickly felt the pain of the stigmata in her body and soul, so much so that she was united with Jesus.

In the same way, Padre Pio carried on his body and in his heart the signs of the Passion of Christ, the stigmata, on his hands, his feet, and his side, as signs of the great compassion of Jesus for sinners. The prophet Isaiah expresses in his passage about the Suffering Servant: *"The punishment that brought us peace was on Him, and by His wounds we are healed."* (IS 53:5) That's how far-reaching the compassion of Jesus is!

However, true compassion doesn't destroy anyone: Jesus' Mother was standing near the cross. Despite his pain, Padre Pio spent hours in the confessional; he didn't spend his time in bed complaining: "Oh, I'm suffering so much!" On the contrary, he worked hard, and sharing in the suffering of others made him rejoice. He was joyful and loved joking with people. True compassion embellishes the soul. If someone is experiencing authentic compassion in his heart, his face radiates light, tenderness, and beauty!

We who want to love Jesus and who want to help Him save souls through prayer and sacrifice, we can ask for the grace of His compassion. To do that, let's present ourselves to the Blessed Mother, the most compassionate of creatures. She is also called the Mother of Sorrows, because she experiences all of our suffering, our illnesses, and our sadness. In the middle of the war in the Balkans, when terrible destruction was taking place in Yugoslavia, she gave us this message: "Dear

Children, your suffering is also mine." (APRIL 25, 1992) She knows when a heart is wounded by betrayal or abandonment; she feels everything.

In this mystery, let's ask Mary, the Mother of Sorrows, for the gift of compassion, the gift of knowing how to cast a benevolent and positive eye on those around us, an eye which doesn't judge, nor criticize, nor focus on faults. An eye which pushes us to act and to offer. May our hearts be able to comprehend what the brother or sister standing next to us sees, what his secret or visible suffering is, and what he endures. Let's learn to resemble our heavenly Father: *"Be merciful, just as your Father is merciful"* (LK 6:36) Jesus, the friend of mankind, tells us! Yes, let's ask Our Lady for this grace.

# The Widow of Naïn and the Resurrection of Her Son

E GO NOW TO Galilee, that same Galilee of Nations in which it is written: *"The people who were in darkness have seen a great light; and upon those who were in that region under the shadow of death, a light has arisen."* (MT. 4:16) We are approaching the little town of Naïn. As always, a large crowd is following Jesus and His disciples. Upon entering the town, they encounter another procession accompanying a widow. (LK. 7:12)

This woman has lost her only son. Jesus observes the funeral procession, which makes its way to the cemetery; He focuses His heart on that poor widow and the tragic situation she is in. Compassion always begins with a gaze. He looks intently at this woman, knowing that she is a widow and has already suffered because of the death of her husband. He knows everything about her. The loss of a spouse is particularly painful; it cuts to the core, because the sacrament of marriage unites the spouses into one flesh for life.

Jesus looks long and hard at her, and what occurs in His heart? It skips a beat with shock. He sees, in advance, His own mother in the same situation: the Blessed Mother has lost her husband, Joseph, and she is at the point of losing her only son. Jesus is profoundly moved. He is the Creator, the One who has created maternal love in a wonderful way: He knows its importance. As the Son of God, He wanted to have a mother on earth: He wanted to be born from a maternal womb; He tasted the tenderness of the love exchanged with a mother; He knew her in the intimacy of a simple household for thirty years.

The compassion that Jesus experiences is unending. He participates in our pain and each moment of suffering in us resonates within Him at an unimaginable depth. When He sees our tears, His heart turns inside out. Later in the Gospel, He will say to Mary Magdalene, who came to the tomb to anoint His body and give Him final reverence: *"Why are you crying? Whom do you seek?"* Before, at Bethany, at the death of Lazarus, Jesus was moved upon seeing the tears of Martha and Mary. Today, Jesus has not changed; He is seized by the same compassion towards us when we lose a loved one.

Faced with this tearful woman, Jesus knows that He has the power to help her, and He goes with haste to do so. He carries within Him the power of the Creator, whose word made our world exist. What does He do? He touches the coffin and says to the young man: *"Get up!"* (In Greek, it is written: "Wake up!"), and He returns him to his mother alive.

When we experience grief, the devil takes advantage of our vulnerability and tries to push us into despair, or at least profound discouragement. He incites us to rebel against God, to doubt His love, and to think that our destiny is unjust. So, the widow of Naïn, deprived of her son, could have thought: "I am older than he is, I should have died before him. He's the only bread winner of the family." When thinking about the departure of our beloved, we, too, can be overcome with anguish about the future, or jealousy of another woman who still has her husband and son. We could be attacked by envy, depression, or a desire to die. But Jesus wanted the widow to avoid these agonies and be given back her son. On His part, His compassion becomes alive, does all that is in His power to do, and offers the best gift. Doesn't He have the power to raise the dead?

Jesus consoles the widow on her great misfortune, but He also offers the young man an opportunity for a second chance. We know that at our death, God will reveal Himself to us as He is. Everything will be exposed in truth, and we will see our lives flash before our eyes like a movie.

The story of an Italian Capuchin, Brother Daniel Natale, who lived in the monastery of Padre Pio in the 1940's, seems appropriate. Infected by a serious stomach disease, Brother Daniel was near death. But Padre Pio, who loved him very much, said to him, "You are not going to die. Go and have surgery at such-and-such a clinic and don't worry!" He was hospitalized and underwent surgery but died shortly after the operation. The brothers told Padre Pio what had happened and understandably he was shocked and taken aback. They told Padre Pio to pray for his life to be restored, which he did, and after a few hours from the death certificate being signed Brother Daniel came back to life.

Of course, he was bombarded with an avalanche of questions about what he had experienced at the moment of death. He explained that, after a sublime encounter with Jesus, he had to go to Purgatory, because he was not yet ready to enter heaven. He added that his greatest suffering came when he realized that he had only achieved part of the plan for sanctity that God had conceived for him, because he had actually been called to great holiness. He was permanently pierced by a sword of sorrow, he used to say to himself, because it was too late to change. But Padre Pio prayed for him and obtained for him the grace of a second chance. Brother Daniel came back to earth, and, after having seen, heard, and lived through his experience of the other world, he radically changed his life, and from then on, he displayed an exemplary charity towards all. Today, his cause for beatification continues: Brother Daniel didn't miss his second chance!

What happened to the son of the widow? When he came back to life, we have every reason to believe that he, too, was able to recount to his loved ones his adventure in the other world, and how different the values of Heaven are from the values on earth! We have every reason to believe that he changed his way of living and used the years of his second chance positively. For, when faced with divine revelation, every man will comprehend one day, the poor as well as the rich, the old as well as the young, the sinners as well as the righteous, that only charitable love endures for eternity and that all the rest disappears like snow in the sun.

Not every parent who has lost a child has the chance to meet Jesus at some corner in the road or to see their child revived. One couple, devastated by the death of their little child, paid a visit to venerable Marthe Robin (a French mystic), hoping to receive a little consolation from her. She said to them: "You are the parents of a saint in Heaven and you are participating in the Redemption of the world." This two fold answer didn't remove the pain they felt, but definitely gave them a taste of Divine joy. A taste of eternal bliss.

It is important to shed light on a confusion which is spreading today in the West. That is the belief in Reincarnation. Now, in the letter to the Hebrews, the question is clear-cut: *"And just as men die only once, after which there is the judgment, so also was Christ offered only once to take away the sins of many; the second time, with no part in sin, He will appear for the salvation of those who await Him* (HEB. 9:27-28).

As for Our Lady, she brought along with her the visionaries Vicka and Jakov to visit Heaven, Purgatory, and Hell. When they returned, she asked them to tell others that after death, there is eternity." *

In another message she states:

> "We go to Heaven as fully aware as we are now. At the moment of death, we become conscious of the separation of the body and soul. It is wrong to teach people that we are reborn several times and that we inhabit different bodies. We are only born once. The body, taken from the earth, decomposes after death. It will never live again. Man receives a transfigured body." (July 24, 1982)

As Father Cantalamessa, preacher to St John-Paul II and to Benedict XVI, declared: "Death is not a wall, it's a door!"

Before asking Jesus and Mary for the gift of compassion for those who have suffered the loss of a loved one, let's consider a type of grief that is prevalent in our times, that of a mother who has had an abortion. It imprints a profound wound on

---

* See: Medjugorje, Triumph of the Heart, Sr. Emmanuel Maillard, 1996, where episodes of this unique journey to another world are explained. Pgs 34 — 36.

the soul of the mother. Having rejected the fruit of her womb to the point of removing it, she will be grief stricken deep in her being and will end up despising herself. Many women who have aborted their children experience a tenacious sadness, which sometimes causes them to consider suicide. In Medjugorje, the Queen of Peace asks prayer groups to show great love to these mothers who have aborted and to make sure that they reconcile with God straight away by making a good confession. Basically, "abortion is a serious sin," she says, "because it is the killing of a human being. Pray, my children, so that such mothers no longer exist in the world!

So many mothers abort because they are motivated by fear or are brainwashed by our culture of death which calls good, evil! So many do it because of egoism or when pushed by a partner or husband who imposes upon them a terrible choice: "It's me or him!" Very often, the pressure is so strong that they reluctantly choose to sacrifice the child, believing that it will keep the father of the child from straying. It's nothing more than a disastrous illusion. How can you ensure the future of a family or establish the unity of a couple over the blood of a tiny, innocent, defenseless being? By making this choice, most women lose both the child and the father at the same time.

Let's open our hearts here with compassion towards these men and women in our disoriented generation! Through prayer, fasting, and sacrifice, and sometimes with words, we can protect life and help these mothers. She who is the Mother of Life will be greatly consoled. The death of a child brings her deep pain.

Let's offer this decade to Mary for the mothers beset by the temptation to abort, as well as for those who have already aborted. May they welcome the grace to love life and for the wounds they carry in their hearts to be healed.

O, Jesus, fill us with Your divine compassion, You who came not to judge, but to save! Give life back to those who are in this world like the living dead, enclosed in the sordid tombs of materialism. Please give them to Your mother, who is also our mother. O, Jesus, bring them back like torrents to a desert, so that our mouths are full of laughter and song!

# *Veronica Wipes the Face of Jesus*

OW WE ARE RETURNING to Jerusalem and slipping into the little group which is accompanying Jesus on the way to Calvary. The story of Veronica, an ancient Christian tradition, rather than part of Scripture, reveals the beauty of the human heart and its capacity to love. It offers us one of the most touching examples of compassion in action. This intrepid woman was prepared to defy the Roman soldiers just to be near Jesus, at her own peril, and to wipe the bleeding face of her Lord. The Church has reserved a feast day for her, February 4, to encourage us to follow her example.

In the writings of the great French mystic, venerable Marthe Robin, we have an inestimable treasure of information on those present at the Passion. Essentially, every week for fifty years, Marthe experienced the Passion of Jesus, in her body and in her soul. She saw its scenes and described them with precision. Marthe affirmed that Veronica is a fictional name which was attributed to her to recall her compassionate gesture. The expression *vera icona*, "true icon, true image," gave us *Veronica*. In reality, her name was Seraphia, a slightly older cousin of the Blessed Virgin, making her an aunt of Jesus.

Seraphia was married to a man of high stature in Jerusalem

and had two children with him. But during the massacre of Bethlehem under Herod, her children were killed, and Seraphia adopted a little girl. She loved Jesus very much; in fact, she adored Him. When Jesus, at the age of twelve, remained in the Temple with the doctors of the law, without His parents' knowledge, it was Aunt Seraphia who brought him something to eat and took care of Him. Unfortunately, when Jesus began His public life, her husband seeing Jesus as an imposter, couldn't stand Him, and forbade his wife from going to listen to Him. (But, it's not all bad news because, after the Resurrection of Jesus, he converted, so profoundly that him and Seraphia became marvelous witnesses in the early Church.)

The interdiction against going to see and hear Jesus was torturous for Seraphia, and, while remaining at home, she tried to obtain news about her dear Jesus. Then came Good Friday. When she learned that Pontius Pilate had condemned Jesus to death, she was like a prisoner in her own home because of her husband, but, from her terrace, she could hear the sound of the lugubrious procession, which was advancing slowly along the *via dolorosa* of Jerusalem. Seraphia burned with one desire, that of rejoining Jesus before He was put on the cross. She could stand still no longer, and, knowing that Jesus would die of thirst, she decided to go and meet Him. What could she do to assuage His suffering? She entrusted to her daughter a bottle containing a delicious alcoholic beverage to quench His thirst. She also took a linen veil to cleanse His holy face, and unknown to her husband escaped from the house with great haste.

She finally joined the procession, but how would she get around the barrier of horses and soldiers armed with lances and chains? How would she reach Jesus? Without even considering the risks of being struck or beaten to death, by some miracle, she ran successfully through the crowd, to get close to Jesus. Love acted; it saw no obstacles; it was not blocked by fear. The little girl, however was not successful in reaching Jesus; a soldier pushed her causing her to let go of the bottle destined for Jesus.

At that moment, Seraphia was standing in front of Jesus looking at Him. In that divine moment between Seraphia and Jesus, that gaze of love which they exchanged was fundamental: it was capable of everything, said everything and contained everything. The Jesus whom Seraphia saw did not appear to be the same Jesus she knew! Perspiring blood in the Garden of Gethsemane, had made His face red. He was wearing the crown of thorns; covered with spit, dust, and even animal excrement. He had fallen several times on the way, and at that time, you could find almost anything in the narrow alleyways of Jerusalem. His swollen face was unrecognizable after the blows inflicted by the soldiers, during His night in prison.

However, the majesty of His profoundly divine gaze mysteriously remained, and, focusing on that sight, Seraphia wiped His face with immense tenderness, cleansing it of the spit, dust, and blood in record time. That was a gesture of perfect love totally inspired by the Holy Spirit! What consolation for Jesus! The prophet Isaiah, who contemplated the Son of God in His Passion prophetically, describes expertly the disfigured face of the Suffering Servant (IS. 53:2-3): *"He no longer had a human face. . . There is no beauty in Him, nor brilliance to attract us . . . He was despised and rejected, a man of sorrows familiar with grief, a man from whom people hide their face, spurned and considered of no account."* Responding to this gesture of perfect love, which gave Him so much comfort, Jesus produced in turn a double miracle: not only did He imprint His divine face on the veil of Seraphia, but He left in her heart a fire of extraordinary love, which would never burn out.

That same linen veil, preserved by the Church for all time, can be found in the Basilica of St. Peter in Rome, under the dome, next to the right-hand column, just under the statue of Veronica. The fabric has darkened since then, but, in 1848, a miracle occurred under the watchful eyes of everyone present. According to tradition, the linen is publicly displayed on Good Friday, but because of the discolor, you could no longer distinguish the face of Jesus. However, in 1848, in an instant the color was restored, and everyone was able to admire the blessed face of Christ for a few minutes, before it darkened again as it was before.

Let's go back to Seraphia. After her act of such courageous love, she and her daughter were pushed back by the soldiers. The child was not able then to bring any relief to the terrible thirst, which was devouring Jesus, torturing Him, and making Him say from the top of the cross: *"I thirst!"*

Veronica excels in teaching us true contemplation: the more she reflected on Jesus, the more her compassion for Him increased. The more she embraced His pain, the more she was transformed by the need to help Him. Oh, if only we knew how much we could help Jesus when we contemplate Him in His Passion with sincere love! Veronica is a witness of it: the more we contemplate Jesus in His *kenose* (in His abasement), the more He transmits to us His divine beauty and the more He imprints on our souls His divine image. How wonderful! The linen cloth has become an emblem of the divine experience which happens when we contemplate Jesus in His Passion. Saint Faustina received this private message from Jesus: "My Daughter, your compassion for Me is a relief; your soul is adorned with exceptional beauty through meditating on My Passion." (DIARY PARA 1657)

Let's not fail to let the Holy Spirit move us in this wonderful way. By contemplating the Passion of Jesus, we acquire beauty, love, and tenderness, and, in the end, we are made divine. Through our gaze of love resting on Him and His gaze resting on us, He transmits His greatest treasures, those famous treasures He cites in Scripture that He wants us to acquire for Heaven. (CF MT. 6:20)

The light drawn from the gaze of Jesus permits us also to recognize Him in the poor, destitute and mentally ill we meet along our way. But don't be fooled. Be vigilant, because this poverty is not only found among beggars, the sick, the handicapped, or the elderly. No, it is also found among the rich, beautiful and seemingly powerful, who have highly recognized social positions, occupations and names. Jesus invites us to be compassionate with all, to the rich as well as to the poor, because, in reality, we are all poor, even if some people don't know it yet. Sometimes poverty tortures the rich more than the poor! We merely have to count the number of suicides among the rich. The sparkly exterior makes the inner distress more insufferable. Think of how many models or movie stars commit suicide! We often don't suspect the interior disarray of those who shine outwardly with their riches and glamor.

In this decade, let's ask Our Lady to look upon us tenderly, and recognize the beauty of a soul in the midst of all its suffering, even its degradation. Let's make an effort to rejoin the soul of Jesus and quench the thirst of His heart.

May Saint Veronica help us through her prayer to look with adoration on Him who, through His compassion towards us, has chosen to lose everything in order to enrich us with Himself. Come, let us adore Him!

# *The Heart of the Shepherd*

E CONTINUE OUR JOURNEY into the life of Jesus, and, in this fourth mystery of compassion, we see Him walking and announcing the Kingdom of God everywhere.

His compassion for the crowds is abundant!

> "And Jesus was going about all the towns and villages, teaching in their synagogues, and preaching the gospel of the kingdom, and curing every kind of disease and infirmity. But seeing the crowds, He was moved with compassion for them, because they were bewildered and dejected, like sheep without a shepherd. Then He said to His disciples, "The harvest is abundant, but the laborers are few. Pray, therefore, to the Lord of the harvest to send forth laborers into His harvest!" (Mt. 9: 35-38)

It is important to remember that Jesus does not look at the crowd in general; He looks at each person individually, the way He created them. "Never forget, Dear Children, that each one of you is a unique world before the Heavenly Father," Mary says (MAY 2, 2016). He knows the potential for sanctity with which He endowed each one of us. With the eyes of His heart, Jesus sees the possibility for these crowds to become holy people, who are one with Him in everything!

The Bible reveals God's great desire for us several times, His dream is always the same: *"You shall be my people and I shall be your God"* (JR. 30:22) Jesus, the Creator, suffers terribly seeing his children wander without purpose, disoriented, like sheep without a shepherd! His heart bleeds, because he knows what they can aspire to if only they are well-guided! Saint John of the Cross complained to Jesus, seeing the great number of believers who were stuck in spiritual mediocrity because of a lack of spiritual direction, when they had in them great potential for holiness. What a shame to waste the gifts from God in that way!

God continuously distributes His gifts freely, but where are those who will receive and accept them? Let's imagine that we are wandering in a desert without water, tormented by a terrible thirst. In this desert there exists a well, but we don't know about it. We have no idea that there could even be one. However, this well is very close to us. This well was dug by someone, therefore that someone knows where it is and how it works. Now that person doesn't say to us: "The well is there; go drink from it; it's free!" So, we end up dying of thirst, only a few meters from the well!

Jesus cured the sick, delivered the possessed, gave back the dignity of people who were held in low esteem, granted sinners a way of finding the state of grace and reconciled them to the Father. All that was truly beautiful, but there is another very important thing: Jesus announced the Good News of the Kingdom to the poor, nourishing the souls with His Word, and teaching widely that Word, which enlightens and gives life. The people who heard Him know this well: *"He was teaching them as one who had authority unlike their teachers of the Law."* (MT. 7:29) Now, this is the same Word that created the world!

Here's an anecdote told in Medjugorje which puts into perspective a genuine fact. In the era of Turkish rule (four and a half centuries followed by communism) in the former Yugoslavia, the government threatened Christians and ordered them to bring their Bibles to the public square to be burned. Many people hid them in their basement and most buried them. From time to time, they joined one another for a ceremony by candlelight. Then, those who knew how to read would take up the Bible and read to others for hours. They nourished the Truth in this way in a hostile environment: drinking from the living water of the Word, which was their joy, their pride, and their strength during that time of trial, in a word, their lives. When the meeting was over, they hid the Bible again, to be taken up later.

In 1981, when the Blessed Mother appeared right in the middle of communist rule, what did she say to them? "Dear Children, I invite you to read the Bible every day and to put it in a visible place in your homes. That way, when someone pays you a visit, you will be able to read a passage together" (OCTOBER 18, 1984). A visible place? After all that had happened? The villagers did what she asked out of love for her and didn't suffer any retribution; the Queen of Peace protected them!

Our Lady appeared several times to Father Jozo Zovko, who was the pastor of Medjugorje when the apparitions began. Five times, she appeared to him in tears, saying with profound sadness: "You have forgotten the Bible!" Father Jozo said more precisely: "She cried with more sadness than a mother who had lost a son. When we forget the Bible, we forget Jesus, her Son, who is the living Word." An essential point in the teaching of Mary in Medjugorje is exactly that: to put the open Bible in a visible place in our homes, to read several verses each day, and to put them into practice.

Today, God still calls a great number of His children to transmit His Word. Observing the present world, one might believe that He doesn't call us anymore, as He did previously. That's wrong! Of course, several decades ago seminaries were full, and parishes had many priests serving the people and now, the shepherds are few, and those who remain are overworked. However, in reality, God continues to call; He calls according to the needs of His children. But those who receive this call today are not always in a position to hear Him. The deafness of the world, the materialism, the attachment and enslavement to material goods, the strong earthly distractions, and the time dedicated to useless things, muffles the voice of the Lord and becomes a soft murmur which is difficult to hear.

Saint Faustina writes in her Diary:

"Silence is a sword in spiritual combat. A chattering soul will never gain sanctity." (St Faustina's Diary, para 477)

"The silent soul is strong; if it perseveres in silence, no vexation will touch it. The silent soul is able to unite itself to God in the most profound way; it almost always lives under the inspiration of the Holy Spirit; in the silent soul God acts without meeting any obstacle." (St Faustina's Diary, para 477)

Our Lady warns us through Mirjana:

> "My Children! Once again, in a maternal way, I beg you to stop for a minute and reflect on yourselves and on the passing nature of your earthly lives. Then, reflect on eternity and the eternal beatitude.
>
> What is it that you want? Which path will you take?" (July 2, 2012)

These are the questions that we ask our heavenly Mother, who sees us engaged and invested in so many vain things! What do we want? What do we desire? Where are we going?

"Today more than ever," says Mary, "Satan is strong; he wants to destroy you and trick you in a thousand ways." (SEP-TEMBER 25, 1990) She speaks to us as a mother, worried to see her children searching for their happiness exactly where it will be lost! Her maternal heart is seized with profound compassion.

Imagine the compassion Jesus feels for the people in our era! They go out to the movies, they follow football games, they stand in lines at malls. They have time for everything, except withdrawing to a quiet place and listening to the voice of the shepherd, who can promise the peace their souls dream of! Jesus is always watching us, whatever we are doing. What's happening in His shepherd's heart? What is He going through? Today is Sunday, and My children are not going to Mass, where I am waiting for them with such desire to satisfy them! If not I, God, then who will fill the emptiness in their parched and wounded hearts, who? They are not receiving the Bread of Life and are even ignoring the fact that I am waiting for them at church!

Yes, God is calling us, but we have become deaf. He is inviting us, but we are afraid of the silence when God is speaking to our hearts, because it is easier to deceive ourselves with the music and noise of the world, which helps us forget the emptiness which haunts us day and night! Through sheer laziness, we drink the lukewarm and empoisoned water of the media, and we pass right by the heart of Jesus, which gives us the water of life.

Who will rise up to give water to our young people, who no longer know who to follow or where to go? Many of them are ignorant about why they were born and what the purpose of their life is! Who will rise up for them, in the heart of our culture of death, to cry out to the tormented and abandoned souls to guide them on the path which leads to Heaven? Who will rise up to announce the Word of God which gives life?

Still today the bleeding heart of Jesus has in front of it an immense, magnificent harvest! His shepherd's heart is overflowing more than ever with the compassion He wants to pour out on each of us. My brother, my sister, rise up, I beg you, rise up! Why do you want to use only 10% of your capacity to love? Why waste your time on foolish things when you could bring the word of God to everyone who is thirsting for it? My very dear friend, Jesus is calling you. He needs you.

In this decade of the Rosary, try to listen to God, because He has a call that's specific to each one of His children. And this very evening, in the silence of your room, say to Jesus: "Here I am, Jesus, what can I do to help You nourish Your sheep? I want to collaborate with You, Jesus! What can I do for You?"

# *The Blind People of Jericho*

N THIS FIFTH MYSTERY of compassion, we continue with Jesus along the well-traveled roads of Judea. A crowd rich in problems, illnesses, and miseries of every kind (MT. 20:29–34) are following Him. They each want to receive from Him a word of comfort, an affectionate glance, or a blessing. What's more, people are saying, it's enough simply to touch Him! He is already a renowned miracle worker, His reputation precedes Him, and each person is nourishing the wild hope that this great prophet is going to look at his particular illness and cure him. The sick, the possessed, the blind, and the lame are all in a state of expectation.

We see Jesus coming out of Jericho, and two blind men sat along the road crying out to Him: *"Lord, Son of David, have pity on us!"* But the crowd doesn't like their shouting and tries to silence them. The blind men begin to yell even louder: *"Lord, Son of David, have pity on us!"* Frankly, the chance of a lifetime has come along. How can they restrain themselves? Jesus stopped, called them, and asked: *"What do you want me to do for you?"* (MT. 20:32) What a splendid question from Jesus!

What would you respond, if God asked you the same

question? What would be your greatest wish? The Blessed Virgin has asked us the same question: "What do you want? Where do you want to go?" The increasingly piercing cries of the blind men touched Jesus' heart. Didn't He come so that the blind could see? Wasn't He Himself the light of the world? Jesus was seized with compassion, because He saw them humiliated by their infirmity. Not only that, the blind and the crippled at that time did not have the right to enter the Temple of Jerusalem to adore God. That law went right back to David. Understandably, these blind men were now making an appeal to Jesus as the son of David! Jesus, moved by their plea, satisfied their request and with a gesture gave them their sight, and, more importantly, restored their fundamental integrity as believers: they could from now on adore God in the Temple!

This episode makes us think of the healing of Malchus, the servant of the high priest, an event which occurred in the Garden of Olives when Jesus was arrested (CF. JN.18:10). When Simon Peter cut off his ear, he became infirm and would be unable to keep his job next to the high priest. As a consequence, he wouldn't be able to support his family. Jesus knew that and cured him on the spot.

When Jesus grants a physical healing there's always more to it than meets the eye, because He touches the soul and dignity of the person and grants a spiritual healing too. How could this servant of the high priest, who had been healed, still be Jesus' enemy? Imagine, also, what was going on in the mind of that high priest, who had felt inclined to arrest Jesus, but was now being told by his servant that he had been miraculously healed.

In the case of the two blind men, as in the case of Malchus,

Jesus performs a double healing: He heals their bodies, and He restores their human dignity. He performs the first healing for the poor who believe in Him and does the second for the enemy who comes to arrest Him. His compassion extends to each person! We have much to learn from Him!

Let's now return to the two blind men. Jesus feels compassion for each person there in the crowd. So, why does He cure only two? That's a mystery which belongs only to God; we can only kneel and adore His will. I think of the questions that so many believers ask themselves, like: why did He cure that sixty-year-old woman of cancer and not cure her four-year-old grandson?

Jesus doesn't see things the way we do. The Heavenly Father sent His Son into the world to save the world for all eternity. How would it serve Him if our bodies are healed, but we perish in Hell for all eternity? The visionary Marija Pavlovic said to me one day: "The Blessed Virgin is sad to see that some people are coming to Medjugorje to ask for a physical healing, but then continue to live in a state of mortal sin." Our Lady affirms that: "No, Dear Children, that's not right, because the health of the soul is much more important than that of the body! You must first renounce sin and make a good confession. There would be many more healings if everyone renounced sin!"

In Medugorje, we see many people renounce sin and testify to their healing upon exiting the confessional. When sight is restored to the blind, they follow Jesus. He has effectively killed two birds with one stone: He cured their blindness and made them disciples. For Him, making them disciples is more important than their physical healing.

However, I often witness a sad reality: some people don't

like the cross and reject it vehemently. Some sick people have such a desire to be healed that they are ready to sell their souls, risking their eternal salvation by talking to charlatan healers or mediums. They mislead themselves by ringing at the wrong doors and spend enormous amounts of money to obtain a cure at any price, to the detriment of their souls. They opt, for example, for seances of reiki, which seem to be offered more and more to the sick, without taking into account that they have allowed themselves to be deceived by a subtle lie, an abomination! They believe they have found a cure, but it is only an illusion, because the masters of reiki invoke demons to treat the sick. The result is that they do nothing but place the illness in another part of the body or psyche, and the naïve victim sees his anxiety increase. The person no longer wants to pray, or casts aside his spouse; he wishes he was dead or even has the desire to commit suicide. This is because the goal of Satan is to destroy us. We encounter victims of reiki often in Medjugorje!

When we ask for a favor from Jesus, that He perform a physical or interior healing, it's important to understand the plan of God for us and to be ready to accept it. The Blessed Virgin has said:

> "Dear Children, when you pray, you keep saying, 'Heal me! Heal me!' No, Dear Children, don't pray like that, because you are concentrating on your problem and are not open to God. Say instead, 'Lord, may Your will be done for me!' Then the Lord will be able to perform a physical healing or a liberation. He knows what He must do." (Message given to Vicka)

On June 23, 1985, the visionary of inner locutions, Jelena Vasilj, leader of a prayer group in Medugorje, received this prayer from Our Lady, who told her that this was the best prayer for a sick person. Here it is:

### PRAYER FOR THE SICK

Oh, my God, this ailing person is before You. He came to ask of You what he desires and the most important thing for him. You, oh my God, let these words enter his heart: "What is important is the health of the soul!" Lord, in everything, may it happen to him according to Your will! If You want him to be cured, may health be given him. But if Your will is otherwise, let him continue to carry his cross. I pray to You also for us who intercede for him; purify our hearts and make us worthy to transmit Your mercy. Oh, my God, protect him and alleviate his suffering, that Your holy will be done in him; that through him Your holy name is revealed. Help him to carry his cross with courage!

At the end, you could say the *Glory Be to the Father* three times.

Before reciting this decade, rather than concentrate on our own illness or that of a loved one, let's look at the heart of Jesus, which always wants the best for us; draw from His gentle gaze the immense compassion He has for each of us. And if He asks, *"What do you want Me to do for you?"* let's make the right choice! Let's not mistake true happiness; let's choose that which begins here on earth and lasts for eternity!

# Mysteries of Mercy

E NOW STAND BEFORE the splendor of God's Mercy! *"Blessed are the merciful, because they will obtain mercy,"* Jesus says (MT. 5: 7). The Beatitudes reveal the true identity of our Savior; they examine His soul like a scanner. Through them, each facet of His personality is revealed, and show the eight reasons why He is happy: He is poor in spirit, meek, afflicted, hungry and thirsts for justice, merciful; pure in heart; a peacemaker, suffers persecution for justice, and is reproached and slandered . . . The sixth Beatitude, that of mercy, shakes our souls to the core and perhaps even frightens us. It's as though it says to us over and over: "If you don't prove that you are merciful towards those who have wounded you, you will not obtain mercy, and you will not reach Heaven." But Jesus didn't come to frighten us. On the contrary, He is showing us the key to salvation! Satan is terrified of mercy, so this key — mercy — is of extreme importance, indispensable in fact, because it's the only way that allows us to vanquish definitively this cruel enemy and his plan of death for us. How do we become merciful? First of all, by imploring it passionately! Then, by contemplating with the eyes of the heart the One who is Mercy Himself, "Look to Him that you may be radiant with joy!" (PS. 34:5).

These five mysteries of mercy will help us forge a new path into the depths of the heart of God. Let's become explorers! Each mystery contains a treasure to discover, to understand, and to integrate into our lives. Jesus' dream is to give us these treasures, and He longs for us to receive them. He passionately wants our souls to reflect His mercy! He will communicate this to us so that we resemble Him. This is the glory of the saints!

In these mysteries, we marvel as we discover what God has revealed is his greatest attribute: mercy. But let's look together at the meaning of the Hebrew word, the one used in the Bible, rather than the etymology of the Latin word *misericordia*. The Hebrew term allows us to understand the profound concept of mercy that God gave His people.

In Hebrew, "mercy" is *rahamim,* the plural of the word *rehem*, which means "the maternal womb," or uterus. It designates, therefore, the most intimate anatomical part of the woman, which is, also, the most beautiful, since it is there that life is conceived, and where the child is formed in secret during the 9 months of pregnancy. It's a place infinitely precious in the eyes of the Creator, a sort of tabernacle in which He collaborates with us in making the spark of life spring forth. Now, when God wants to explain His mercy, He uses this word, but in the plural, *rahamim.* Of course, it does not mean that God has several wombs, rather he uses the plural to emphasize the intensity.

# The Prodigal Son

ET'S BEGIN WITH THE parable of the prodigal son, in which Jesus gives us a wonderful image of the Heavenly Father (CF. LK. 15:11-31). A son demands his independence, takes up his belongings, his money, his inheritance, and leaves the father's home, where he was born. In that moment of unconscious blindness, this young man is convinced that his independence will bring him great happiness, but it is a trap set by the Evil one, and he falls into it. The father's heart is wounded and bloodied. He knows that his son is the victim of a great illusion, that he wants to follow his whims away from the watchful eyes of his father. He desires freedom and independence and in his naivety, is unaware that his choice will make him the slave of his perverted and blind nature. He destined himself for complete failure. He will be humiliated, bankrupt and starving. He will be obliged to become a caretaker for the pigs — a situation which is not Kosher! Such a humiliation for a Jew!

What's the problem here? Why such a miserable end? This son has chosen to be a free electron, a disconnected satellite; he seeks fulfillment far from the presence of his father, because he hasn't understood that beside his father, he has everything, most importantly love and the beautiful horizon that love gives. He makes himself an orphan the moment he removes himself from everyone in the house. What a contrast there is between the cold decision of the son to leave and the immense tenderness of the father, who, with a broken heart, watches the son travel far away but keeps a look out for him every day as he scrutinizes the horizon!

It's the same with us. The closer we come to the Holy Trinity, the more our communion with the three divine persons increases. On the other hand, the more we distance ourselves from those three persons, the more we lose peace and become free electrons completely detached from God. The Blessed Mother teaches us that our lack of peace originates in us moving away from God. That distance which separates us is the favorite territory of the enemy, where he can act against us in perfect tranquility. By contrast, our union with God deprives him of his field of action!

How does God react to this? He gives us the freedom to choose whether to accept Him or reject Him: it is the son who decides to distance himself from his father, not the contrary. In the Father's heart, the place once occupied by this son remains empty.

This creates a distressing gulf between them. The father waits every day for this very beloved son, and, like a sentinel, he hopes the son will return to fill the empty place in his heart. Of course, the father could be bitter and think: "He's the one who wanted to get out of here. Too bad for him! Let him live his life; I won't think any more about him!" Not at all! The father waits for his son, and he continues to wait every day by the side of the road. Here is divine mercy; here is the depth of the maternal womb, here is someone who could not stand to see his child go, knowing full well that, if he went far away, he would lose everything: happiness, peace, joy, communion, life! The mercy of God is like the deep love of a mother. Every mother can understand that!

We see that the son became a watchman for pigs and that he suffered from hunger, but . . . What was he thinking during these difficult moments? "I was better off at my father's house." He decides then to return to his home, not because he loved his father, but because he was hungry. We really have to recognize the reality of his motivation! In any event, at the end of the day, he came to his senses and returned. . .

How does the father react when he spots him in the distance? He runs toward him! He welcomes him warmly and embraces him effusively. This prodigal son stinks, because a man who travels so many kilometers after having lived with pigs would surely not smell like roses! But his father doesn't even think about that. What does it matter to him? His son has returned. It's a miracle! He doesn't even give him time to finish his confession. He clasps him with infinite tenderness and delicateness, with extraordinary joy! It's so beautiful! His paternal heart is overflowing with love! Straight away he gives orders to his servants to prepare a feast: "Kill the fatted calf, put a ring on his finger, dress him in the finest robe, and let's celebrate together." (LK. 15:23)

I think back to that day when Sister Faustina Kowalska committed a sin. She was very ashamed of it; she experienced profound regret, and humbled herself before God. But Jesus helped her to understand that by humbling herself in that way, she was gaining more grace for her soul than if she had not committed the sin.

God is so good that He takes our sin, and, if we return to

Him, instead of condemning and chastising us, He transforms the sin into something positive. Sin is bad; it stinks. But when someone repents out of love for Jesus, He transforms that sin into perfume, as the Heavenly Father said to Saint Catherine of Sienna. (THE DIALOGUE OF ST CATHERINE OF SIENNA)

Saint Maryam of Bethlehem offers us a wonderful comparison that is good to hold onto, because it is a source of healing for the tormented soul: "In Heaven, the most beautiful trees are those which have the most sin. This is because they use their misery as manure and place it at the foot of the tree."

The sinner understands that God can change his sin into something wonderful. He leaves his sin at the foot of the tree, in the same way we spread manure, to enrich the earth and allow the tree to produce beautiful fruit.

During this decade of the rosary, let's allow ourselves to embrace our Heavenly Father, without mulling over our errors! As serious as our sin may be, let's cast it off into the burning heart of God: the Father is waiting.

# *Jesus and the Samaritan Woman*

IN THIS MYSTERY OF mercy, we are visiting Samaria. Jesus visits Jacob's Well during the hottest part of the day, and He sees a woman there. Jesus, having the knowledge of hearts, knows her well, and knows that she is a lost sheep. He starts to speak with her in an attempt to save her. (JN. 4: 1-30)

He knows that this woman has had five husbands and that she is currently living with another man. Searching for love she changes partners several times. All in vain! Her thirst to love and be loved, her desire to find a lasting love has now become an open wound. This woman is dying of thirst, that insatiable thirst for love never found. Jesus began with a question and said to her: "Give me a drink!" What a magnificent introduction! By explaining His own thirst, Jesus made Himself similar to her and joined her in her fundamental problem. In reality, Jesus thirsts to save His lost sheep, and she, on her part, was thirsty for love. These two were made for each other!

But the woman did not understand that Jesus was talking about the thirst of His heart. She couldn't even imagine that He was bursting with compassion for her, because she thought her life was a total failure and that there was no way out. Basically, she had lost her reputation as well as her own self-esteem. What future could she hope for? Was happiness possible for her? Hadn't she already played all her cards? Seeing the distress of this woman, Jesus burned with an immense desire to recover His lost sheep, to bring her back to her marvelous vocation as a woman, and to restore her original beauty. He wanted to bring her out of the pit of despair which was holding her captive and restore her splendid identity as a woman created for love and fruitfulness.

Jesus helped this woman understand that, to fully quench her thirst for love, she had to stop running from one meaningless relationship to another, and start to adore God. Yes, adore! Jesus did not condemn her. On the contrary, He revealed to her how to obtain the one and only true love which can fully satisfy the human heart. He makes her an adorer of God. The woman was no longer a prisoner of her bad choices, and, from that moment on, she would no longer seek happiness in places where that happiness gets lost. It is in the adoration of the true God where the living water flows, the water which irrigates everything by its own passage. Jesus explained further, that if she drinks the water springing from His heart, she will never thirst again: "Everyone who drinks this water will be thirsty again, but whoever drinks the water I give them will never thirst. Indeed, the water I give them will become in them a spring of water welling up to eternal life." (JN. 4: 14)

That applies to us too, as we often feel anxious, desolate, troubled, frustrated, empty . . .When we adore Jesus in the Blessed Sacrament, and also adore God in spirit and truth in nature, we are irrigated by that bounteous river which overflows from the heart of Jesus. The desire for that love we aspire for from the deepest part of our being is finally satisfied and we feel content.

It is Jesus' miracle of mercy, which transforms mankind, or, rather helps them become themselves, to recover their true identity as creatures of God. The mercy of God reveals to us who we really are.

This woman, who was scorned by all those living in her village, is transformed by Jesus into an adorer and an evangelist. Here her vocation of fruitfulness is realized! And what fruitfulness! God chose her to bring salvation to her whole village, she who was the most despised of all! Such is the mercy of God: the smallest in the eyes of men, the one whom no one would choose, becomes the elect. Thanks to her, the entire village recognizes and believes in Jesus! Jesus liberated her from the shame which burdened her and made her an entirely new person, a bearer of the true light for others. Then, the joy of having become an instrument of God healed her wounds.

During this decade of the rosary, while we are contemplating the heart of Jesus, which is overflowing with living water for us, let's put into His hands all our frustrations, our emotional failures, our unrealized desires . . . Let's open ourselves up to Him! Aren't we all thirsty? Jesus is standing here, right in front of us, ready to give Himself entirely to us. Now, let's drink from His heart!

# Jesus and the Adulterous Woman in Jerusalem

OR THE THIRD MYSTERY of mercy we are present at an upsetting scene. It's morning in Jerusalem and Jesus has come down from the Mount of Olives, where He has spent the night praying. Today, as He does every day, He is teaching in the Temple, surrounded by a group of people listening intently to His words. The Pharisees and the Scribes bring to Him a woman who has been caught committing adultery. They drag her in front of Him, and, therefore, before the whole crowd! What lack of respect on their part! What humiliation for her! But why are they acting like this? They certainly don't intend to take care of this woman, and of her soul, alas, that seems to be the last thing on their mind. Their goal is, rather, to trap Jesus, and they are using this woman, to incite Jesus to say something against the law. They observe that Jesus loves sinners, and that He wants them to truly repent. They deny His mission as Savior, because jealousy blinds them and prevents them from adhering to Him!

They have worked out an *almost* perfect scheme against

Jesus to trap Him. On the one hand, they plan to provoke Him about the most crucial part of His mission: to bring back to God the lost sheep of the House of Israel; on the other hand, they plan to confront Him on the Law of Moses, an incontrovertible law, which is to stone women like that. Jesus cannot transgress Holy Scripture. It's very evil on their part! Certain of trapping Him, they ask:

> "Master, this woman has just now been caught in adultery. And in the law, Moses commanded us to stone these women. What, therefore, do you say?" (Jn. 8: 4-5)

Jesus, the living Word of God, reacts in a surprising way: He stays quiet! But He begins writing on the ground. The Scribes and Pharisees are waiting for Him to say something; they are disconcerted, even irritated. They persist in questioning Him. Then Jesus raises His eyes and says: *"Let he among you who is without sin cast the first stone!"* They remain quiet, petrified, and no one moves. As for Jesus, lowering His eyes again, He continues tranquilly writing with His finger on the ground. What could He be writing? Their curiosity is stirred, these masters of the Torah approach Him, one by one, perplexed.

We know that Jesus is God and He knows how to search the hearts of men. How have these so-called intelligent masters not yet understood Him? Jesus waits in silence, head bowed, in order not to upset the sinner. He has just written on the ground the most serious sin of the first one among them who approached Him. The man reads his sin and is afraid! Here is his sin, known and spelled out! *"But who is this man who knows my life so well?"* he says to himself. *"And what if the others discover it?"* Ashamed and trembling, he leaves that place as quickly as possible. But Jesus, watching the other nosy ones arrive, does not want the sin of the first to be known by the other Pharisees. He does not follow their example, of taking pleasure in publicly exposing the sin of the woman. He allows His divine mercy to shine through. From the hand of the Creator and Savior, He erases the sin of this man. Disappeared, finished, wiped off the map! Here is the Lamb of God, Who takes away the sin of the world! Another Pharisee comes up but has no way of knowing the sin of his brother. The seal of the confessional is saved!

What sensitivity Jesus shows the sinner! He didn't want to bring shame to the sinner, so He didn't reveal his sin to anyone. That's why, in Saint Faustina's faithful image of the merciful Christ, Jesus has His eyes lowered. The most well-known image does not show this, unfortunately, but it is what the saint described.

Let's stop for a minute and contemplate the manner of Jesus, the gentleness of His love for the sinner. He even wants to save the person who takes pleasure in accusing others! Didn't we feel a certain joy, knowing that Jesus had written their sins in the soil? Weren't we tempted to think: "Serves them right!" Jesus suffers when faced with any sin; He bleeds internally. Being united to Him means we too feel the pain of the sins of others, even if those sinners seem unrepentant. What became of those Scribes and Pharisees? We don't know. Did they by any chance understand that Jesus was offering them the opportunity to do the right thing and renounce the sin living inside them? Would they still reproach Jesus for showing His mercy?

In the Gospels, we see the men all leave, one after another, beginning with the eldest, those who had undoubtedly committed the greatest number of sins. Once everyone is gone, Jesus raises His eyes, and, noticing that the woman is still there, says to her: *"Woman!"* just as from the height of the cross, He would say to His mother: *"Woman, here is your son!"* By the name Jesus gave her, He returned to the adulterous woman the wonderful dignity of creation, the woman of the sixth day created in the image of God. *"Woman, where are they? No one has condemned you?"* Trembling with hope, she asks herself how He, this Man so meek, was going to react towards her. She knew the law: there was no pardon for female adulterers! She answered: *"No one, Lord!"* *"Then, neither do I condemn you,"* Jesus said to her. Just imagine the relief of the woman! She had gone from a condemnation of certain death to total liberation. Total? Yes, but, from now on, she had to stop breaking the laws of God because Jesus hadn't forgotten to say firmly: *"Go, and sin no more!"* (JOHN 8:11) Let's hope that she understood that sin leads to death. Wasn't that a fortunate escape? *"The wage of sin is death,"* St. Paul tells us, *"but the gift of God is eternal life in Christ Jesus Our Lord ."* (RM. 6:23)

It's beautiful to see that the heart of Jesus, like our own at this moment perhaps, is close to the female victim of this evil hypocrisy. He liberates her from the danger of death and invites her to find the state of grace once more and change her life. However, what surprises us more is that the heart of Jesus considers the destiny of the proud as well, the men who consider themselves righteous, by erasing their sin with His own hand. They were all pardoned; that's why they left without saying a word, reduced to silence by this totally unexpected mercy. They would not quickly forget this Jesus of Nazareth and His surprises! *

I want to emphasize one thing: we are all champion slanderers, because when we see or learn that someone has sinned, we don't waste any time divulging it and spreading gossip, thereby ruining the reputation of our brother. Here is an anecdote from Saint Philip Neri, a saint who had a heart for sinners. One day, a woman went to confession, and, among other things, she confessed that she had told some slanderous lies. Instead of giving her absolution right away, Philip Neri said to her: "Go to the market, buy a chicken, and bring it to me." She obeyed. Philip then said to her, "Now, return to the market square, and pluck the chicken." And she complied. After having plucked the chicken, she returned to see Philip Neri, and said, completely content, "I did what you asked." He responded, "My daughter, return to the market square, and gather up all the feathers that you pulled from the chicken." But she said worriedly, in response, "That's impossible with this wind. The feathers have blown everywhere. I can't catch them all again!" And the saint explained to her, "Of course! Now you understand what you've done: a lie told about someone cannot be erased. It's out of control; it begins to propagate and make its own path of destruction." And the woman, sincerely repentant, finally received absolution.

Let's return for a minute to the female adulterer, who had broken an important commandment of God. In His great goodness, through the intermediary, Moses, God gave us the Ten Commandments to help us discern between the good

---

* According to a vision of Marthe Robin, cited by Father Finet, her confessor, during his retreats.

which gives life, and the evil which brings about death, and
invites us to observe them:

> "Keep His statutes and commandments, which I give you,
> that it may be well with you and your children after you, and
> you may live a long time on the land which the Lord your
> God will give you." (Dt.4:40)

> "A curse, if you do not obey the commandments of the Lord,
> but turn aside from the way which I now show you and walk
> after strange gods which you know not." (Dt.11:28)

> "All these curses shall come upon you, and pursue you, and
> overtake you until you perish, because you did not hear the
> voice of the Lord your God and did not keep His com-
> mandments and statutes, which He gave you." (Dt. 28:45)

It goes without saying that if we want to have life within us,
we must observe the commandments that came from God
Himself. Giving children catechism books that don't contain
the ten commandments anymore is putting them in grave
danger, and you can see the results of that! They are not
receiving the indispensable compass required to direct them
to the light of God in the middle of a world which bombards
them with false lights.

The Blessed Mother is clear on this point: if we ask for
her help, let's do it in a consequential way. We can't implore
her and then not take into account the word of God, as
though she can act independently of the plan of God: "Dear
Children," she says, "I cannot help you if you don't live out

the commandments of God, if you don't live the Mass, if you don't reject sin." (OCTOBER 25, 1993)

But, be careful! The Evil One is today setting a subtle trap, and many of our contemporaries are falling into it! There exists a certain demon who is enjoying stunning success in the world. His name is "Everybody does it." Let's take the example of a married woman who is tempted to sleep with another man. Having received a Christian education, she knows that this is a grave sin which will offend the Lord, and, if she commits it, she will no longer be able to receive Jesus in Holy Communion. She feels a strong attraction towards this man, but she also doesn't want to risk committing a serious sin. The Spirit of God, through the commandments, will enlighten her. But what is the evil spirit going to keep repeating? "Don't worry. Everyone's doing it." If everyone's doing it, it must be good, so, why not me? There's the trap. Pay attention, because everything that opposes the word of God is a lie! I have used this very common example because within our life spans, we have seen so many people anguished, broken, even suicidal because of this demon. Even if everyone else is doing it, I don't want to do it; I don't want to betray my Lord by conforming to the world around me! Jesus never said, "Do what others do!" He said, *"Follow Me!"* It's an entirely different choice.

In this mystery, let's contemplate the merciful heart of Jesus, wounded by the sin of man. But from that wound flows a river of pardon for all who desire to return to Him. Let's pray with all our hearts: "Jesus, You are magnificent! You are everything to me! You are the true love I want to fill myself up with; You are all I want in my life! You love me completely; no one will ever love me the way You do! You created me; You breathed Your life into me; You protected and saved me; You spilled Your blood for me. To whom would I go to obtain true happiness if not to You, Jesus? With sincere humility, I welcome Your mercy, and I contemplate Your heart. Make my heart resemble Yours, Jesus; pour into it all the abundance of Your mercy! Didn't You say: *"Blessed are the merciful, for they shall receive mercy"*? (MT. 5:7)

# *Jesus and the Good Thief*

N THIS FOURTH MYSTERY, we are with Mary at the foot of the cross where Jesus has been crucified and we are contemplating our Savior as He lives His last few minutes. It is fundamentally important that we continue to contemplate Jesus; it's the best disposition to have in all circumstances. Jesus is in the process of giving up His lifeblood, drop by drop, while suffering terribly. His right shoulder is completely dislocated from the brutal stretching done by the executioners to make His hand reach the hole in the wood where it was to be nailed. His flesh is pierced by the nails and the crown of thorns. Two other men, criminals, are crucified with him. On one side, one of the thieves speaks to Him, rebelling, and refusing to accept his death. He attacks Jesus by sniping: *"If You are the Christ, save yourself and us too!"* (LK. 23:39). He expected, perhaps, to see a true miracle which would allow all three of them to come down from the cross!

The attitude of the other thief is completely different; unknowingly he is soothing the heart of Jesus and consoling Him. How? This man was also a wrongdoer, a villain with a long list of thefts and murders to his name; he was no angel, because to undergo the pain of crucifixion, he must have committed serious crimes. In spite of his life as a thief, he turns toward Jesus and looks at Him. Their eyes lock. The gaze of Jesus exudes majesty, despite the agony of the cross, and the thief understands little by little that Jesus is no ordinary man, He is the Son of God, the King of Israel!

Despite his sin, the heart of this criminal is open to goodness and grace. The gaze of Jesus resting upon him produces an illumination of conscience and has already transformed him. At the brink of death, he detaches himself from the evil which has been inhabiting him, to the point of reprimanding the other thief: *"Do you not even fear God, seeing that you have the same condemnation? We are punished justly, for we are getting what our deeds deserve. But this man has done nothing wrong."* (LK. 23:40-41). This criminal has become Jesus' advocate; he is truly the only person who is speaking up for Jesus during His passion! For our Savior, this must be an immense consolation. Jesus is in the process of giving up His life for sinners, that is, for me, for you, for us all, and who is at His side? A sinner to whom He can offer salvation immediately! In this good thief He sees immediately the fruit of His Passion. Certainly, the heart of a sinner, but a sinner who doesn't hesitate to invoke the aid of God. By recognizing the evil that has been committed, he is opening himself up to mercy.

When Jesus hears these humble, sincere words, *"Jesus, remember me, when You come into your kingdom,"* filled with joy and admiration, He immediately gives the man the keys to Heaven: *"Amen, I say to you: this day you will be with me in Paradise."* (LK. 23:42-43) He makes this thief the first saint, canonized by Jesus Himself, despite his appalling history! The Church venerates him today under the name of Saint Dismas. That's extraordinary! Jesus is incredibly happy to have found a sinner who accepts His sacrifice, who welcomes the fruit of His passion, and who falls to his knees humbly before Him: "Lord, I need You; I can't get there alone; I need You; remember me!"

Consider this scene for a moment: the humble attitude of the man is unleashing God's torrents of mercy. Let's keep that in mind: the humility of the sinner who sincerely recognizes his sin and repents of it sparks at that very instant the immense tenderness of God, always ready to erase a sin, even the most serious one. The wrongdoer experienced this. The heart of Jesus is a fiery furnace which burns sins and makes them disappear. If Saint Dismas is, according to the Church, the first saint, canonized by Jesus Himself from the height of the cross, we, also, must have for everyone, especially those who have committed the most horrible sins, full confidence in the mercy of God. "Mercy is drawn from the vase of confidence," (ST FAUSTINA'S DIARY, PARA 1602) Jesus said to Saint Faustina! Without this confidence, how could we return to Him without fear and ask pardon with all our hearts?

Let me recount for you the experience of a dear religious friend who lives in New York, where the most formidable prison in the entire United States of America is located. It holds the most dangerous prisoners, those who have committed the worst crimes. These men suffer greatly, because they are imprisoned for life in narrow cells which resemble rabbit cages, empty and without light. They grow weary thinking about death and fill themselves with all kinds of dark thoughts. A sort of Hell for which death is the only exit!

This particular nun was not afraid; she went to visit them to give them some comfort, with the help of the angels, armed only with the word of God and His mercy. From their tiny, barred cells, they cried out when they saw her: "What is this nun doing in this hell?"

One day, speaking with a prisoner who was vaguely recalling some basic Christian teaching learned in his childhood, she said to him: "You know, you can still receive the mercy of Jesus; you mean so much to Him! He loves you. He's calling you. He's waiting for you to give you His forgiveness! Go to Him! Don't hesitate!" The prisoner, shocked, answered her, "Are you kidding me? What are you telling me? I can still go to Heaven? Me? I won't go to hell?" "No," she said, "If you ask for forgiveness from Jesus with all your heart, He will be very happy to forgive you, and you can go to Heaven." "Go to Heaven, you're joking," he answered, "That's impossible. You don't know what I've done!" But she insisted: "Believe me, Jesus loves you as you are, and He wants to erase all your sins. You just need to say to Him: Lord, forgive me! That's all." And he said, "That's incredible!"

When the visit was over the nun headed towards the exit, but when she was still in this sordid hallway, she heard him cry out to another prisoner in a neighboring cell: "Mo! Mo! Guess what the nun told me! I can still go to Heaven! Do you believe it? I can go to Heaven!!" Howling with joy, his voice resounded throughout the whole prison. He had understood that he could still be saved, he, the horrible criminal, and it was so simple: sincerely ask pardon from Jesus! He could have shouted this good news to the whole world!

"When a sinner turns towards my mercy, even if his sins are as black as night, he brings me the greatest glory and does honor to my Passion." (ST FAUSTINA'S DIARY, PARA 378)

If we take into account the splendor of the heart of Jesus and the depth of His mercy, we would throw ourselves blindly into His arms. The depth of His mercy is endless, so what are we afraid of? What's holding us back? It is our lack of confidence in His mercy! Jesus said to Sister Faustina: "The distrust of souls tears at my heart, but the defiance of one chosen soul does even greater harm. In spite of the mercy that I have inundated it with, it still distrusts me." (ST FAUSTINA'S DIARY PARA 50).

What does the devil whisper to us? "It's too late. You have done too much. Stop dreaming. God is not even going to give you a second thought! You have no chance. Give up. You're just going to anger him more!" So many sinners allow themselves to be convinced by these venomous words; some even go as far as refusing to see a priest on their death bed. Let's never forget that Satan is jealous of the possibility of conversion and the return to the loving heart of Jesus that is offered to us on earth. Satan detests the mercy which tears away from him the souls that he had succeeded in seducing. It steals them away, even from his most sordid dens. God always wants to give us another chance, one more opportunity to grab on to, as many as a hundred times each day, without dwelling on our pitiable state . . . God is magnanimous!

My Friends, while praying this decade, let's fix our eyes on the loving gaze of Jesus, so that He may transmit to us, as He did to the Good Thief, the same warmth of love and the same mercy. Let's put aside any sentiments of guilt or self-judgement. Let's approach without fear this river of love which invigorates the soul, which purifies and transforms us, which brings us peace, serenity, and joy. We have the opportunity right now to look at Jesus, and, in the warmth of our hearts, strive to bring to Him the same joy the Good Thief offered to Him on the cross.

# Peter's Denial

ERE WE ARE AT the last mystery of mercy. I want to conclude with a wonderful episode, (LK. 22: 54-62) when Jesus, tied up with chains, silently gazes at Peter after his triple denial. Those involved are Jesus, Peter, several servants, and a rooster. For the Jews of that time, the rooster was a very important animal, because it signaled the end of the night and the dawn of a new day. In this passage of Scripture, the rooster symbolizes the passing of the darkness of human misery to the light of divine mercy.

At the Last Supper, Jesus announced that His end was approaching and that He would be betrayed. We can empathize with Peter, who resembles us to a large extent, when he spoke out with conviction: *"Even if I should have to die with You, I will never deny You!"* (MT. 26:35) In Peter's defense, let's not forget that everyone declared the very same thing at the Pascal meal!

Peter was sure he loved Jesus, and it was true that he loved Him very much; but he was forgetting his own miserable state of being and limitations. The love of Peter for Jesus was human and, therefore, limited and self-centered. Peter was certainly touched by the tenderness of Jesus, and by His unique way of guiding them, the way of a good shepherd, not hesitating to share the most difficult details of their daily life. Peter appreciated the treasures that he received from the Lord he loved, because this was an influential, powerful, and fascinating man. Basically, Jesus knew how to speak to the crowds like no one else: He shut down the cynics, performed extraordinary signs and miracles and was responsible for incredible events; this was truly a fantastic man! Peter was proud to follow Him, to belong to His clan and to be its head, as designated by Jesus Himself.

But the hour of trial had arrived, and Jesus appeared to His apostles in a totally different way. In the Garden of Olives, Peter saw the face of his hero covered in blood, weakened, and the worst thing was Jesus did not put up any resistance to the group of Judases who had just arrested Him. He behaved like a miserable defeatist, allowing Himself be put in chains. Peter was thunderstruck; he didn't understand anything anymore. What was happening? Even in this dramatic situation, he still showed himself to be a man of great courage and began to follow Jesus in order to know His destiny, even from afar, while the other disciples escaped right away.

Peter entered the courtyard of Caïphas and drew close to the fire, because it was cold that night. Jerusalem is 800 meters high up and this was the beginning of April. Around the fire, someone recognized him and said: *"This man was with Jesus of Nazareth."* (MT. 26:71-72) And Peter denied it: *"I don't know this man."* Then, another person declared loudly and strongly the same thing, and again, Peter denied it. An hour went by between the second and third denial. One hour? That felt like an eternity when he had denied the One who had become the center of his life! During that hour, Peter suffered; he had lost everything; he had ruined everything, and he was drowning in his misery. The devil doesn't waste any time; he took advantage of this weakness, of this cold, and of this fear to push the chief apostle towards sin. What happened to that beautiful promise of never abandoning Jesus? How had this robust, intrepid man lost his courage?

Peter had not yet realized the extreme depth of his misery. He was convinced that he loved Jesus because of his own strengths and capacities. Now, he felt desperate, because he didn't have the courage to say: "Yes, I know Him; I'm one of His." His beautiful dream was demolished in one hour, those three years spent near Jesus, obscured. And he was going to deny Jesus again! But he hadn't finished speaking when the rooster began to crow; it was the signal that Jesus had prepared to awaken His apostle Peter from the depth of his misery; the rooster obeyed the Lord and crowed! Peter remembered, then, the words Jesus had spoken at the Last Supper: *"Amen I say to you: this very night, before the cock crows, you will have denied Me three times."* (MT. 26:34) At that precise moment, Jesus fixed His gaze on Peter. There was a sublime moment when the eyes of the Savior rested upon the eyes of the sinner, upon the person who had denied Him. My God! It was at that moment that Peter found again the Jesus he knew, the Master, Prophet, Love Incarnate, Mercy . . . He received right in his heart this gaze of love and mercy, of compassion and gentleness. Then, he departed quickly from this courtyard of darkness and went out to weep bitterly. Peter loved Jesus and cried for having pierced the heart of the One he loved.

From then on, Peter would never be the same. He was aware of his misery, of the limits of his own love, of the bravado which masked his lack of courage: he no longer recognized himself. He believed himself to be a strong man, chosen by Jesus for his leadership qualities, the one who had said, under the inspiration of the Holy Spirit: *"You are the Messiah,"* in short, the one Jesus could count on. But here he was, broken, empty, wounded to the very depths of his being . . . completely ruined!

However, just at that moment in which he discovered his shame at the triple denial, Jesus transmitted His immense mercy with a silent gaze, without even a shadow of reproach. This was a unique moment in the story of redemption. The misery of the first pope became a springboard to attain a completely different level of love! Yes, from then on, Peter would love Jesus with humility; he would love Him as never before. Peter cried out of love, not despair. For him a new life began, because from then on, Peter would follow the Master by making himself as tiny as a child, relying only on divine grace rather than his own strength.

Beginning with that loving gaze, after the tears had fallen, Peter became Saint Peter, because he had left all his misery inside the heart of Jesus; he felt pardoned and loved even in his poverty. He became Saint Peter, the split stone on which Jesus would found His Church, yes, a split stone which recognized itself as such. Jesus didn't want to found His Church on illusory human strength, but on His mercy. My dear friends, we are all damaged, split, sinners, but we have Jesus with us. He doesn't let go of us nor reject us in trials of truth; He is the Savior who knows our misery and wants to take it upon Himself, to transform it into divine love.

When Jesus revealed Himself to Sister Faustina, she was already very close to God and very advanced in holiness; but one day Jesus said to her: "My Daughter, you have not given me what's essentially yours." Surprised, she wondered what she had not yet given, because she sincerely believed that she had given Him everything: her life, her youth, her health, her meager belongings . . . But Jesus clarified it: "My Daughter, give your misery over to Me, because that belongs to you exclusively." (ST FAUSTINA'S DIARY PARA.1318) She was expecting anything but that! Don't we give God the best of what we have? What interest would God have in a tainted gift? Sister Faustina was convinced that you only offer beautiful things: sacrifices, little privations, prayers, fasts, praises, works of charity, but not what was pathetic, wretched, or foul. Now, that's exactly what Jesus wants us to give to Him; He needs our misery as the prime ingredient for transformation, by divine mercy and love. His treasures rise up as high as Heaven, but what He wants from us is the only thing that truly belongs to us.

How do we give our misery to God? Through confession! When we confess, we give to Jesus all our limitations and our failures, and Jesus waits for us there to fix His eyes on ours, with immense compassion as He did for Peter on that night.

"Dear Children, I beg you, give the Lord all your past, all the evil that has built up in your hearts. I want each of you to be happy, but with sin, no one can be happy. So, Dear Children, pray, and in your prayers, you will discover a new path. Joy will be felt in your hearts. Thus, you will be joyful witnesses to the things that my Son and I accomplish . . ." (FEBRUARY 23, 1987)

After His resurrection, Jesus didn't say to Peter: "Listen, Peter, I love you very much, and I have made you king of the Apostles, but you have denied me three times in front of everyone, so I've changed my mind, and I'd rather have John.

He was also in the court of Caïphas, but he didn't deny Me. What's more, he was at the foot of the cross. You understand, then, why I have to go back on my promise?" No, the gifts of God are without compunction, irrevocable; and Peter became a much better leader after these events. By becoming aware of his weakness, he was capable of understanding the weakness of every man and that of the Church. He did not judge arrogantly the scandalous behavior of certain priests who were prisoners of sin. No, he understood, because he, also, had behaved scandalously.

Peter and Judas are not differentiated because of the types of sin they committed, denial and betrayal are both grave sins; the difference is that Judas missed his rendezvous with Jesus' gaze. When he handed over his Master on the Mount of Olives, Jesus looked at him; Judas gave Him a kiss on the mouth, but his attention was concentrated on his treacherous plan. All he had to do was meet the gaze of Jesus, Who was ready to forgive him for everything, as He had done for Peter. One word would have been enough. He would have returned, like Peter, and we would have Saint Judas!

And today? When we sin and begin to commit the same sin time and time again, let's not ever focus on our misery, because the devil takes advantage of that by suggesting: "It's obvious that you will never get there. You're nothing but a loser. What are you doing right now with all the graces you've received from Jesus? It's all hopeless, so let it go!" That's his method. Discouragement. But Jesus, one way or another, always has "a little rooster" that He can arrange to crow in our dark nights, in order to remind us that He is with the sinner, and that it's never too late to throw ourselves into His arms.

During this decade, I invite you, one more time, to fix the

eyes of your heart upon the gaze of Jesus, Who is our refuge, our salvation, our beatitude, our Heaven! We want to remain there, to be one with Him, and to fill ourselves up with His mercy. That way, we can become apostles of His mercy, not through our own poor strength, but uniquely through His divine presence in us and through His grace. Let's raise our eyes to Jesus right now! Let's become what we contemplate: let's become mercy!

"Whoever looks at Him will radiate with joy!" (Ps. 34:5)

# Appendix

# The Queen of Peace

"Your prayers touch me deeply and especially your daily Rosaries" (25ᵗʰ January 1982).

"Meditate every day on the life of Jesus and my life by praying the Rosary" (8ᵗʰ August 1982).

"Dear children, let all the prayers you say in your homes in the evening be for the conversion of sinners because the world is in great sin. Every evening pray the rosary" (8ᵗʰ October 1984).

"I would like the people to pray along with me these days. And to pray as much as possible! And to fast strictly on Wednesdays and Fridays, and every day to pray at least one Rosary: the joyful, sorrowful and glorious mysteries" (14ᵗʰ August 1984).

"The Rosary is not an ornament for the house, as it often happens. Tell everyone to pray it" (18ᵗʰ March 1985).

Once Marija Pavlovic asked her: "What do you want to say to the priests?" and Our Lady replied: "Dear children, I invite you to call on everyone to pray the Rosary. With the rosary you shall overcome all the adversities which Satan is trying to inflict on the Catholic Church.

All you priests, pray the Rosary! Dedicate your time to the Rosary!" (25th June 1985, 4th anniversary of Our Lady's apparitions).

"Dear children, put on the armor for battle and with the Rosary in your hand defeat him! Thank you for having responded to my call" (8th August 1985).

"Dear children! Today I call you to begin to pray the Rosary with a living faith. That way I will be able to help you... Dear children, I am calling you to pray the Rosary and that your Rosary be an obligation which you shall fulfill with joy. That way you shall understand the reason I am with you this long. I desire to teach you to pray" (12th June 1986).

"Pray and let the rosary always be in your hand as a sign to Satan that you belong to me" (25th February 1988).

"Take the Rosary and gather your children, your family around you. This is the path to salvation. Be an example for your children" (2nd February 1990).

"Dear Young People, Satan is strong and will try to do everything to bother you, hindering all your endeavors. Therefore, increase your prayers because you need it in these last times. The best weapon against Satan is the Rosary" (1st August 1990).

"God has sent me among you so that I may help you. If you so wish, grasp for the rosary. Even one simple rosary can work miracles in the world and in your lives" (25th January 1991).

"Dear children, I need your prayers now more than ever before. I beseech you to take the Rosary in your hands now more than ever before. Grasp it strongly" (18th March 1992).

"Dear children, I invite you to pray in your family or in your community, the glorious mysteries in front of the Cross for my intentions" (9th September 1995).

"I call all priests and religious brothers and sisters to pray the rosary and to teach others to pray. The rosary, little children, is especially dear to me. Through the rosary open your heart to me and I am able to help you" (25th August 1997).

"When you are tired and sick and you do not know the meaning of your life, take the Rosary and pray; pray until prayer becomes for you a joyful meeting with your Savior" (25th April 2001).

"Pray that you can be apostles of the divine light in this time of darkness and hopelessness. This is a time of trial. With a rosary in hand and love in the heart set out with me. I am leading you towards Easter to my Son" (2nd March 2012).

"Your prayers directed to me are the most beautiful roses of love for me. I cannot but be where I sense the scent of roses" (2nd February 2017) "To me, my children, give the gift of the rosary, the roses which I love so much. My roses are your prayers pronounced with the heart and not only recited with the lips. My roses are your acts of prayer, faith and love. When my Son was little, he said to me that my children would be numerous and that they would bring me many roses. I did not comprehend Him. Now I know that you are those children who are bringing me roses when, above all, you love my Son, when you pray with the heart, when you help the poorest. Those are my roses" (2nd December 2017)

"The most wonderful thing is when a man kneels down with the Rosary in his hands, because the Rosary beads are a weapon stronger than a nuclear bomb" (Message given to Jelena's prayer group and shared with the pilgrims).

# What the Saints say

PADRE PIO, THE HOLY FRIAR FROM PETRELCINA, used to pray the Rosary unceasingly, holding the Rosary in his hand as a powerful weapon which "will obtain for him everything!" Our Lady promised him this. He used to say: "Pray the Rosary, always pray it, as often as possible".

"The Rosary is my favorite prayer. A wonderful prayer! Wonderful in its simplicity and in its depth". This is what Padre Pio said about the Rosary. The Capuchin friar understood the importance of the Rosary after praying hundreds and hundreds of them.

Moreover, to those who asked him why he prayed so many Rosaries every day, he replied: "If Our Lady has always insisted on the Rosary everywhere she has appeared, don't you think that there must be a very special reason?"

On another occasion, he said that he had seen from the window of the choir a square full of demons shouting: "Die! Die! . . . ". So, he turned to Our Lady asking for help and She put the Rosary in his hands to be used as a weapon. He went to the window with the Rosary in his hands and saw all the demons falling to the ground.

Padre Pio used to prepare for Mass by waking up at 1 o'clock in the morning, praying the Divine Office and many Rosaries. Until 4.50am he let Our Lady prepare him for Mass and, as he wrote, Our Lady herself with her indescribable motherly tenderness brought him to the altar.

Once someone told him: "Father, some people say that the Rosary is now outdated, in fact in many churches it is not prayed anymore". Padre Pio immediately replied: "Satan always tries to destroy this prayer, but he will never succeed: it is the prayer of She who triumphs over everything and everyone. It is She who taught it to us, in the same way that Jesus taught us the Our Father". One night Padre Pio told the friar who helped him to go to bed: "Boy, before you go, take the weapon from my pocket". The friar, very surprised indeed, looked in the religious habit of Padre Pio, to check if there really was a weapon. Padre Pio insisted: "Keep looking 'cause it must be there". The friar didn't want to contradict him so he put his hand inside the pocket of Padre Pio's habit and then confirmed: "Father here there is just the Rosary, there is no weapon" and Padre Pio replied: "And is that not a weapon?"

SISTER LUCIA OF FATIMA. In 1957, Sister Lucia wrote to Father Fuentes: "The Most Holy Virgin in these last times in which we live has given a new efficacy to the recitation of the Rosary to such an extent that there is no problem, no matter how difficult it is, whether temporal or, above all, spiritual, in the personal life of each one of us, of our families, of the families of the world, of the religious communities, or even of the life of peoples and nations that cannot be solved by the Rosary. There is no problem I tell you, no matter how difficult it is, that we cannot resolve by the prayer of the Holy Rosary. With the Holy Rosary, we will save ourselves. We will sanctify ourselves. We will console Our Lord and obtain the salvation of many souls".

In 1970 Sister Lucia wrote to another nun: "The Rosary is the prayer of the rich and the poor, of the educated and the simple: take this devotion away from souls, and you take away their spiritual daily bread. It is what sustains the little flame of Faith that has not quite been extinguished in many consciences. Even for those souls who pray without meditating, the very act of taking up the Rosary to pray is already a remembrance of God, of the Supernatural. A simple recollection of the mystery of each decade is one more ray of light to sustain in souls the still-smoldering wick. This is why the devil has made such war against it. And what is worse is that he has succeeded in deluding and deceiving souls who have great responsibility because of the positions they occupy! They are the blind leading the blind!"

In October 2001 Sister Lucia said to all the Marian Communities in the world: "Our Lady asks us to pray her Rosary with more faith, more fervor, contemplating the Joyful, Sorrowful and Glorious mysteries of her Son who chose to include her in the mystery of our salvation. It's when the Rosary beads move in your hands that the Angels and the Saints join you. Therefore I urge you to pray it in deep concentration, with faith, meditating with religious reverence the meaning of its mysteries . . . Pray it in private or as a community, at home or outside, in church or in the street, with simplicity of heart, following the path of Our Lady with her Son. Pray it always with deep faith for those who are born, those who suffer, those who work and those who have died. Pray it in communion with all the righteous in heart and all the Marian Communities, but above all, with the simplicity of the little ones whose voices join the voice of the Angels. Today more than ever the world needs your Rosa ry . . . Many times the prayer of the Rosary has placated the rage of Divine Justice, obtaining mercy for the world and salvation for many souls". Also: "The decay of the world is without a doubt the consequence of the decay of the spirit of prayer. It is because of this confusion that Our Lady has insisted on the prayer of the Rosary. The Rosary is the most powerful weapon to defend us in battle".

St. John Bosco. The greatest pedagogue of young people considered the Rosary one of the foundations of his educational teaching. Once Marquis Roberto D'Azeglio went to visit the Oratory and was very impressed with the work of Don Bosco. However, he criticized the fact that they prayed the Rosary which he considered a useless and boring practice that should have been suppressed. Don Bosco replied with both kindness and firmness: "Well, to me this prayer is really important, to the point that I could say that all my work is based on the Rosary; I would give up many other important things but not the Rosary".

Don Bosco tried to instill the love for the Rosary and for this mission he found encouragement in his dreams. In 1862 on the eve of the feast of the Assumption he had a dream which revealed the power of the Rosary.

He dreamt to be back in his village, in his brother's house, with all his children. All of a sudden, the Guide who was with him in his dreams appeared and told him to go to the meadow next to the courtyard, where there was a huge snake, 7 or 8 meters long. Don Bosco was horrified and tried to run away. But the Guide told him not to be afraid and stay. Then the Guide took a rope and told Don Bosco: "Take this rope and hold it tightly from your side; I will hold the other side and we will hang the rope over the snake". "And then?" "And then we will bash it on its back with the rope". "Ah! No, please! Poor us if we do this. The snake will attack us violently and rip us into pieces". The Guide insisted and reassured him that the snake would not hurt them; Don Bosco agreed to do what he was told. The Guide, in the meantime, lifted up the rope and with it gave a powerful lash on the reptile's back. The serpent jumped in the air turning his head to bite who was hurting him, but it got caught in a sort of slip-knot. "Hold tight" — shouted the Guide — "and do not let the rope go" and went to tie his side of the rope to a pear tree nearby. Then the Guide took Don Bosco's side of the rope and fastened it to the bars of one of the windows of the house. In the meantime, the snake was struggling furiously, hitting the ground with its head and its coils so violently that its body was tearing and pieces of flesh started to fly off. The scene carried on until the only thing left was its skeleton. Once the serpent was dead, the Guide untied the rope from both sides, folded it and closed it in a small box. After a few moments he re-opened the box and, to the amazement of the saint and the children, they saw that the rope took the shape of letters forming the words: 'Ave Maria'. The Guide explained: "The serpent represents the evil one and the rope the Hail Mary or rather the Rosary, which is a series of Hail Mary's, with which one can fight, win and destroy all of Hell's demons".

Shortly after, Don Bosco saw a heartbreaking scene: he saw some children picking up the pieces of flesh of the serpent, eating them and being poisoned by them. "I could not find peace — said Don Bosco — because in spite of my warnings, they kept eating. I shouted at one of them and then I shouted to another; I smacked one, I punched another, trying to stop them from eating, but in vain. I was beside myself, when I saw all around me a great number of young people lying on the ground in an appalling state". Don Bosco asked the Guide: "Is there anything that we can do against all this evil?" "Yes". "What is it?" "The only thing is the hammer and anvil". "Do you mean I need to put them on the anvil and hit them with the hammer". "The hammer — replied the Guide — represents Confession, the anvil represents Holy Communion: it is necessary to use these two tools".

Cure of Ars. Once he was invited to preach the Spiritual Exercises to the people in a village not too far from Ars. The first thing the Cure of Ars asked the parish priest was whether among the parishioners there was someone willing to pray intensely. The priest pointed to a poor beggar, who was only good for praying lots of Rosaries. The holy Cure of Ars immediately approached the humble lady and asked her to pray the Rosary continuously throughout his sermons. The lady did what she was asked. The Spiritual Exercises were very successful. The number of conversions was extraordinary and the Cure of Ars said with joy: "This is not my work, but that of Our Lady beseeched by the beggar with her Rosaries".

SAINT THÉRÈSE OF LISIEUX. The Saint of the Little Way, of spiritual littleness, confirms that, no matter how terrible men's sins are, "With the Rosary one can obtain anything. It is like a long chain that ties together Heaven and earth; one side is in our hands and the other in the hands of the Holy Virgin. As long as people pray the Rosary, God will not abandon the world, because this prayer is very powerful and touches His heart. The sweet Queen of Heaven cannot forget her children who, without ceasing, sing her praise. The Rosary rises like incense to the feet of the Almighty. And Mary sends it back to us like salutary dew that restores our hearts. There is no prayer that pleases the Lord more".

SAINT JOSEPH CAFASSO tells us that one day, very early in the morning, he met in the streets of Turin an old lady who was clearly in deep concentration. The Saint drew near to her and asked: "How come, my dear lady, you are about so early?" "I am cleaning the streets". Surprised by the answer, our Saint asked: "What do you mean?" "Tonight is the Carnival, and people commit a lot of sins. That is why I walk and pray the Rosary, to cleanse the streets from so many sins".

SAINT MAXIMILIAN MARIA KOLBE. In the Diary of this great contemporary apostle of Mary, we read this short statement: "So many Rosaries, so many souls saved".

Saint Pompilio Pirrotti. An extraordinary Apostle of the Rosary for Souls in Purgatory. With his Rosaries, he became very well acquainted with the Souls in Purgatory, who showed to him their gratitude for the comfort they received from his Rosaries. This familiarity got to the point that when he prayed the Rosary you could hear the Souls praying the second part of the Hail Mary's.

Saint Mother Teresa. "Hold on to the Rosary like the ivy holds on to the tree, because without the Virgin Mary we cannot go forward".

FATHER GABRIELE AMORTH. He passed away in 2016, and was probably the best-known exorcist in the world. In the introduction to his last book "Il mio Rosario", he writes: "I believe that the Rosary is the most powerful prayer, after the Mass and the Liturgy of the Hours". In this last book, when he was 90 years old, he revealed the source of his inner strength: the daily prayer of the Rosary with the meditation of the 20 mysteries. This is the prayer that sustained him in his daily battles against evil, during his work for the Diocese of Rome.

CARDINAL ERNEST SIMONI. He is nearly 90 and during the communist regime he was sentenced to death several times. He spent more than 20 years in prison doing hard labor in the sewers. In 2017 during the Youth Festival in Medjugorje he said: "All those who pray 3 Rosaries every day will experience unimaginable miracles. Therefore, love the Rosary and pray it. I can assure you that Our Lady, the Queen of Peace, will shower you with many graces and you will receive light and peace. Everything you ask Our Lady, she will present to Jesus and Jesus will grant you. Today I want to testify to this, right here in Medjugorje and in these very days. Do not be afraid, She is with us and will always protect the world!"

# Testimonies

Hooray for the Queen of the Rosary! Some religious communities are forced to close for lack of vocations. A sign of the times? What if there was a solution? A very simple one . . . I give you a significant example:

We are in Quito (Ecuador) in 1982 . . . The Carmel was called "Carmen Alto", very poor, it was about to disappear because they didn't have any vocations. The nuns were all quite old and therefore the novitiate had to be closed. No vocation was on the horizon and that was the situation they had been going through for a few years now. The Prioress, Mother Maria Elena of the Heart of Jesus heard about Medjugorje and started to hope again. A religious lady from Italy belonging to the Comunità Dorotea, sister Luicela, one day went to see her to tell her that she was going to Medjugorje with a group of pilgrims. Immediately Mother Maria Elena asked her to pray in Medjugorje for vocations to her Carmel and also to try and meet with one of the seers who could pass this petition to the Most Holy Mary. Moreover, knowing that one could write a letter to the Virgin Mother and that She would answer her request in her heart during prayer, she wrote a letter and entrusted it to sister Luicela. By the way, the Comunità Dorotea was also suffering from a lack of vocations.

Sister Luicela didn't manage to meet any of the seers;

nonetheless she had the opportunity to be at a public apparition. When the seer told the crowd what Our Lady had said during the apparition, the nun was shocked! Here is the actual message: "All communities who will pray every day the full Rosary (meaning 15 decades) for the intentions of my Immaculate Heart, will be looked after by me personally and I will choose their vocations".

When she returned from Medjugorje, sister Luicela passed the message to the Prioress of the Carmel who felt deep in her heart that the message was directed to her personally. At the beginning she wasn't sure what "the intentions of my Immaculate Heart" meant, but then she understood: "It's all clear! The intentions of Our Lady are the intentions of God!"

During the Chapter * of the Community, the Prioress asked the nuns to pray every day the 3 parts of the Rosary (meaning 15 decades), and the religious community happily agreed to do so. They changed the timetable of their daily routine in order to introduce this duty and they also prayed while working. A period of great Marian fervor started in the community. Within a few months they had their first vocation, with sister Mary of the Angels, and then others followed. The

---

* A Chapter may be held at a general, provincial or local level depending on the structure of the religious community; whether general, provincial, or local, Chapters have a long and respected history within vowed religious life. The term "chapter" originated with the early monks who gathered daily as a community to listen to a reading from the Rule of St. Benedict. Little by little this gathering of the monastic community became known as "the chapter" of the monastery and the place where it met the "chapter hall".

vocations were so numerous that the Prioress was forced to open another Carmel, the one of Santo Domingo in Ecuador.

And when they became more than 21 nuns (which is the maximum number allowed for a Carmel), they had to open another one in Panama. On the 23rd January 2017 the first Carmelite nuns arrived in Santo Domingo in Panama. More than five hundred worshippers, priests and nuns attended the blessing of the Carmel by the local bishop, Monsignor Manuel Ochogavia together with the bishop of Santo Domingo, Monsignor Bertram Wick. It goes without saying that in these Carmels they still keep the tradition to pray every day the three parts of the Rosary!

During my mission in Galilee in April 2017, the nun who told me this story at the Carmel of Haifa, sister Maria Lorena, disclosed: "As for me, I am one of the fruits of Mary's messages and of these prayers, because I entered the Carmel of Santo Domingo!"

A few years ago, Mother Maria Elena went to visit a Monastery of Poor Clares who, after they heard the story, decided to do the same and pray the three parts of the Rosary for vocations as asked by Our Lady. Needless to say, that after a while, new vocations were granted to the Poor Clares!

Now we can understand the reason why the Gospa so often reminds us: "Dear children, I invite you to live my messages!" At the moment, for the Church and the entire world there is a lot at stake. We mustn't neglect any of the weapons we have. May this gift, which Our Lady of the Rosary has given us, inspire a renewal in her discouraged children. The Most Holy Mary never disappoints.

# Mrs. Siemienska's Rosary beads

ADAM CHMIELOWSKI, at the age of 24, was already a famous painter. Handsome, young, rich, and a go-get ter, "he had everything going for him," to use that most treacherous saying in the world. At the end of the 19<sup>th</sup> century, Warsaw's high society was snapping up his paintings, and his success promised him a brilliant career. A Catholic by family tradition, Adam was upright and honest, but he had begun to shift toward some very dubious, even occult, practices. Some evenings he would join his wealthy friends in Krakow who would invite him to practice Ouija boards and communicate with the invisible world. In the middle of the Siemienski's extensive living room was a large table made of extremely heavy wood with weighty metal rods. The kind of table that is ideal for these activities where "spirits" are called upon, and where they respond by making the table leap and bound as if it weighed no more than a feather. Adam was fascinated!

However, in a remote corner of that dark room, someone was suffering. It was Mrs. Siemienska, the wife of the medium. A devout Catholic, she knew the Bible and was aware of how displeasing her husband's activities were to God. Does Scripture not clearly state that this is an abomination before

Adonai, the Living God? * However, she wanted to stay in her corner and pray, hoping that her petitions would counter any evil spirits and curb the damage they could do to these lost souls. Her Rosary in hand, she prayed the decades, begging the Blessed Mother to intervene.

But now, the spirits were manifesting forcefully! The heavy table began to twist and turn in the living room. Her warrior blood began to boil, she didn't care anymore! Brandishing her Rosary, she leapt up, walked toward the group of spiritualists, and angrily threw her Rosary beads on the table. Wide-eyed, dumb-struck and bewildered, Adam watched. Under Mrs. Siemienska's Rosary, the heavy table immediately stopped turning and broke in two! Adam later testified: "We heard a sound like a gunshot." Frightened, the spirits turned on the light, bewildered. A deathly silence ensued . . . Adam had just experienced the shock of his life. He stared at the little Rosary beads lying next to the wretched broken table, like David's little pebble near the paralyzed body of the giant Goliath. He

---

* "When you come into the land that the Lord your God is giving you, you shall not learn to follow the abominable practices of those nations. There shall not be found among you anyone who burns his son or his daughter as an offering, anyone who practices divination or tells fortunes or interprets omens, or a sorcerer or a charmer or a medium or a necromancer or one who inquires of the dead, for whoever does these things is an abomination to the Lord. And because of these abominations the Lord your God is driving them out before you. You shall be blameless before the Lord your God. For these nations which you will dispossess listened to soothsayers and diviners; but as for you, the Lord your God has not permitted you to do so. (Deut 18: 9-14).

understood it all. That was all he needed: In this battle between good and evil, the Blessed Mother had defeated Satan with a simple Rosary! From then on, his life changed radically: he turned his back on his wealth, his successes and his dubious activities in high society. He transformed his art, started painting the face of Christ, and began to serve the poor. He even went to live among them, in the sordid neighborhoods of the outcasts and thieves of Warsaw.

He would preach to them the Good News of Christ and make them disciples. He founded a religious order, the Albertine Brothers. His example of charity, his miracles, his compassion for the poor and his holy foolishness in imitating Christ became so remarkable that he enjoyed another form of glory, this one being divine and everlasting. Adam, aka Brother Albert, returned to the Father in 1916 on Christmas Day, at the age of 71, and his fellow Pole, Pope John Paul II made him a saint on November 12, 1989.

And what about Mrs. Siemienska? She probably only discovered the fruit of her Rosaries and the sufferings she offered up when she reached heaven! On that day, in the corner of her darkened living room, how could she guess that her husband's illustrious friend, this brilliant young Adam, would be defeated by her simple Hail Mary's, whispered in the secret of her heart, to the point of becoming a saint? How could she hope that she would one day see the power of Mary victorious over the forces of evil before her own eyes?

# Family Memories...

## MY GRANDMOTHER

Even at the age of one hundred, my grandmother never failed to pray her Rosary every day. But one evening, while I was praying with her, she confided to me: "You see, my darling, I do say my prayers (her Rosary). However, I have to admit that when I am done with them, I'm happy! I don't have that joy in prayer which you have. And that worries me! I should feel joy when I pray because God is good!" I reassured her and promised to pray for her in Medjugorje so that she could experience joy in prayer. She too was to ask for this grace from Mary.

A few months later, I went back to Paris and visited her. I couldn't wait to ask her whether she now prays the Rosary with joy. She looked at me, delighted, and said, "Well, my darling, it's happened! It was worth waiting a hundred years to receive this grace!" We had simply joined our voices, even at a distance, and asked Our Lady for this favor . . . It's never too late, even if you are a hundred years old!

MY FATHER

During the Second World War, my father was arrested by the Gestapo for his activities in the Resistance. He spent three years in a cell with 10 other resistance fighters in concentration camps in Germany. As a great lover of Our Lady, he prayed the Rosary often. His mother, whose only son he was, had no news of him during those years, but she was heroically trusting in Mary, and kept believing that he would return, praying rosary after rosary.

One day when my father was exhausted and starving like all his fellow prisoners, the SS on duty asked the prisoners to carry stones from a quarry to the place where they planned to build something. Each prisoner was given a stone to carry. When my father saw the stone he was given, he understood that his last hour had come, for it was impossible for him to lift it even an inch as it was so large. He also knew that if he didn't carry it, the dogs of the SS would jump on him and the guards would finish him off like a beast. He had seen this happen before.

Standing by his stone, in his distress, he looked up. He then saw a simple house close by, and on its façade was a small alcove in which stood a statue of the Blessed Mother. When my father saw the statue, he exclaimed inwardly, "Mary, save me!" At that very moment, the heavy stone became weightless! My father used to say, "It became lighter than confetti!"

Of the 10 men in his Resistance cell, he was the only one to come back alive (thanks to which I was born!). Needless to say, my father never failed to pray his rosary every day!

NOTHING IS IMPOSSIBLE WITH GOD!

Missions far away always open up unexpected and unsuspected horizons! One of my best experiences in Argentina was when I visited a men's prison in November 2018 — one with high security, because it was reserved for notorious criminals.

More than ten years ago, two men decided to lift these prisoners out of despair, show them God's love and lead them toward a profound conversion. When I came to the prison that day, I found men who were smiling, peaceful, considerate of one another . . . I couldn't believe my eyes! It was a long love story that enabled these two evangelists to introduce the Rosary prayer to this prison. The Blessed Mother did wonders in their hearts.

I will never forget this visit! When the door opened for us to go, we didn't want to leave these prisoners who had become our brothers. We went to evangelize, but we were the ones who were greatly evangelized by these men whose lives had been shattered and who, thanks to the prayer of the Rosary and the maternal love of the Blessed Mother, became extraordinary witnesses to the power of Christ's resurrection.

Let me give the floor to Damien, the shining light in this incredible story . . .

"When your home phone rings at 6.35 in the morning, you can be sure that it won't be to give you good news. Our daughter Lucia, 19, remained calm, despite the situation. On her way to University that morning, she had a terrible car accident. Nina, another 19-year-old girl, was driving her motorcycle in the opposite lane, and apparently fell asleep after working all night in a gas station. She crossed into the other lane, and crashed into the front of Lucia's car, right in the middle. At first, she appeared dead, lying in a pool of blood, with her leg strangely twisted because of multiple broken bones. Lucia tried to talk to her, but Nina was unresponsive. Then she moved a finger and just barely regained her senses when the ambulance came to take her to the hospital. The helmet had definitely saved her life, and most probably so had God.

My wife Josefina and I rushed to the scene of the accident. It was a mess. Lucia was incredibly mature considering such a terrible incident. The cars started parking, and soon there was a traffic jam. Passersby made the sign of the cross as they slowly walked by, staring at the remains of the accident. Thank God Nina recovered from the accident after a series of surgeries and is now the mother of a beautiful little boy.

One of the cars passing by was Coco Oderigo's, who was driving his eight children to the same school we send ours. "Damian! Are you in this mess? Is something wrong? Is anybody dead? Let me drop the kids off at school and come back to help you with some legal advice here." I cannot thank Coco enough for this. His expertise as a criminal lawyer saved us from having to deal with highly complicated legal issues. However, one morning I met him while he was dropping his kids off at school.

— Coco, I need to talk to you. I am very anxious as to the outcome of these legal issues. Do you have time to grab a cup of coffee this morning?
— Sure! Why don't you follow me?

We were fairly good friends with Coco, and our kids were friends as well. We shared the same family and religious values and saw each other at Mass on Sundays. We really cared for each other. However, that morning he was driving the car a little bit "off the beaten path" for just a cup of coffee. But then, he was the boss, so I simply followed. The road became really nasty, and all of a sudden, I was heading toward a barrier. And this was not a country club we were entering! We parked the cars next to a huge mass of grey concrete with barbed wire on top.

— What is this???
— This is a prison

I had never been to a prison, and least of all a prison built on a landfill. This was definitely not a coffee house!

— I know you well enough to see that you are going to like it. I have been teaching rugby to prisoners for four years now. And I told them that today, I was going to bring them a professional motivator to give them a speech . . . but the guy didn't come. So, why don't you start thinking about what you are going to tell these guys? Give me your ID, we are going inside the prison.

I only had fifty meters to walk and think about what I was going to say, and no clear idea came to my mind. Coco was right, deep inside I liked this. There was no other way Coco could have dragged me to a prison. No time to think or react. I had to just jump in! The next minute I had 13 dirty scoundrels in rugby clothes stood around me, in an appalling field, introducing themselves with the most gracious nicknames. They were "Los Espartanos". "Liebre (Hare). Diente (Tooth).

Piojo (Louse). Simpson. Chino (Chinese). Pupi . . . " and on
and on. I talked about the values of rugby, the importance
of teamwork, the 18-year-old Uruguayans who crashed with
their plane in the middle of the Cordillera de Los Andes, and
how rugby helped them survive 72 days in that cold prison
with no food or water.

I never forgot those first hugs I received . . . It was a mystery . . . It was as if I represented the freedom they longed
for, and the warm hug I received that morning from each
one of them was their only contact with the free world out
there. It was a very touching experience. I remembered the
souls in Purgatory for a moment because it is similar to jail in
the sense that you can do nothing to improve your situation.

After a few months, I told Coco that I wanted to go back
to Penitentiary Unidad 48 and visit them. I really missed them.
He came up with the idea of organizing a spiritual retreat in
the "Pabellon 8", the Rugby block.

— We can get a few speakers, you give a lecture, now that
you are a "professional motivator", and a priest to say a Mass
and a closing speech. Done!

That is Coco. He just pushes you all over the place and we
follow, meek and obedient. My speech that day was about the
prayer of the Rosary. How it impacted my life. As a boy, my
memory was very vivid, thirteen brothers and sisters kneel-
ing beside my parent's bed, praying the Holy Rosary to the
Blessed Mother. That is how deep my Irish family roots go,
both from my mother and father. My house was pretty much
like a prison, especially if you were among the youngest kids,
like myself. Bullying, injustice, never enough money, food or

clothes, being a slave to your elders, and all kinds of Human Rights violations, to put it in a hilarious perspective. And a lot of work. Nothing made sense despite having incredibly generous parents, who gave their lives for us. But as a little boy, I was very selfish and could not understand why I had so many brothers and sisters, and so little comfort, especially compared to my friends! But when we prayed the Rosary at night, there was a special grace that fell from Heaven, and everything was transformed. Everything made sense. At that moment, peace was all around, and my parents were the best. And guess what? I loved my brothers and sisters! We ended up playing with each other! Not fighting! And it was very clear to me that all this came from praying the Rosary as a family.

When I formed a family with Josefina, I adopted the same tradition, and the same grace came to us. It became especially true when I received the news that my youngest son Michael was diagnosed with Duchenne Muscular Dystrophy, DMD. I had a positive spiritual shock at that very moment, I sensed that every Rosary and every Mass I had ever attended made itself present in that instant. And a gentle voice said, "It was all for this". So that, in a nutshell, was my speech that morning. I bought 40 Rosaries and gave one to each of the inmates, along with a little book "How to pray the Rosary" and kissed them goodbye. But . . . I realized no one knew how to pray the Rosary. Many were unable to read or write. So, I decided to go back the following Friday and pray an entire Rosary with them, so they could continue praying on their own from then on.

The following Friday, Coco and I showed up with some delicious cookies, enough for 40, and started teaching them how to do it. The mysteries. The decades. When the cookies ran out, there were only three or four well-educated inmates who stayed until the end. There was no real interest. "Will you come back next Friday?" I wasn't sure if this was for the cookies, for me, or for the Rosary, but I didn't want to know the answer either.

So, we went back, and the same thing happened. Friday after Friday. Then some friends and people who had attended spiritual retreats started asking about the possibility of joining in prayer with Los Espartanos. We also started noticing that more and more Espartanos gathered in prayer, and the effects I had experienced in my own family became evident once again. The Pabellon 8 was turning into a pleasant place to be. It started feeling more like a home. Like a family. Like friends. And every time a Rosary ended, there was peace and joy all around. Now all the Espartanos were praying, and "people from the street" (so they called us) started coming in growing numbers. Between one Mystery and the next, we had discussions about forgiveness, healing of the soul, tenderness, love, childhood, carrying the cross, Satan's work, the Resurrection, lives of the Saints, eternal life, and a variety of intentions. We started praying for "our Pope's intentions", for our families, for the sick, for the poor. Coco then suddenly said "Let's visit the Pope", and one year later, ten "Espartanos" who had recovered their freedom after serving their sentence, together with twenty volunteers, sat in Santa Marta at the Vatican for an hour and a half with the Holy Father.

The graces of the Blessed Mother were and continue to be abundant. We have witnessed conversions, miracles, healing . . . and continue to be surprised Friday after Friday at this work that Mary started more than five years ago.

To cut a long story short, in this Penitentiary Unit 48,

every Friday, some 300 inmates pray the Rosary with devotion in "Pabellones 7, 8, 10, 11 and 12". The prayer of the Rosary has never been interrupted: neither the summer, Christmas, Easter, holidays, the winter, the cold, the rain, or extreme hot weather have ever stopped the prayer. It has now expanded to the prison next door, Penitentiary Unit 47, as well. And more and more prisons where rugby started, are followed by the prayer of the Rosary. Every Friday, the inmates await with great expectation the arrival of "people from the street" to pray the Rosary. More than one hundred volunteers pack the parking lot every week and wait their turn to get into the prison and pray to Our Lady alongside the inmates. She pours her grace over us, sending us back home with our batteries fully recharged.

We are front-row privileged witnesses of her work, and as Pope Francis said, "The Blessed Mother transforms a cave of animals into a house of Jesus, with a few rags, and tons of tenderness". We keep saying that phrase, and the inmates reply "Prisons used to be caves of animals, with violence, death, pain and suffering . . . but here where we play rugby, and where the Rosary is prayed, they are no longer caves of animals . . . this is a house, a club, and you are welcome anytime".

I'm so glad Coco didn't take me to a coffee house on that day! It feels so good to be part of a team that has become an instrument for the Most Blessed Virgin Mary!

DAMIAN DONNELLY, ATTORNEY
*Buenos Aires, Argentina*

# The 15 Promises of Our Lady made to Blessed Alan de la Roche

1. To all those who shall recite my Rosary devoutly, I promise my special protection and very great graces.

2. Those who shall persevere in the recitation of my Rosary shall receive a sign of my grace.

3. The Rosary shall be a very powerful armor against hell; it will destroy vice, deliver from sin, and dispel heresy.

4. The Rosary will make virtue and good works flourish, and will obtain for souls the most abundant divine mercies; it will substitute in hearts love of God for love of the world, and will lift them to the desire of heavenly and eternal goods. How many souls shall sanctify themselves by this means!

5. Those who entrust themselves to me through the Rosary, shall not perish.

6. Those who shall recite my Rosary devoutly, meditating

on its mysteries, shall not be overwhelmed by misfortune. The sinner shall be converted; the just shall grow in grace and become worthy of eternal life.

7. Those truly devoted to my Rosary shall not die without the Sacraments of the Church.

8. Those who recite my Rosary shall find during their life and at their death the light of God, the fullness of His graces, and shall share in the merits of the blessed.

9. I shall deliver promptly from purgatory the souls devoted to my Rosary.

10. The true children of my Rosary shall enjoy great glory in heaven.

11. What you ask through my Rosary, you shall obtain.

12. Those who propagate my Rosary shall be aided by me in all their necessities.

13. I have obtained from my Son that all the members of the Rosary Confraternity shall have for their brethren the saints of heaven during their life and at the hour of death.

14. Those who recite my Rosary faithfully are all my beloved children, the brothers and sisters of Jesus Christ.

15. Devotion to my Rosary is a great sign of predestination.

# Indulgence

A plenary indulgence may be gained:

1. Devoutly recite the Marian rosary in a church or oratory,
   or in a family, a religious community, or an association
   of the faithful, and in general when several of the faithful
   gather for some honest purpose;

2. Devoutly join in the recitation of the rosary while it is
   being recited by the Pope and broadcast live by radio or
   television.

In all other circumstances the indulgence is partial.

To gain the plenary indulgence one must pray the rosary as
detailed above and must be free of all attachments to sin,
even venial sin. Three other conditions must be fulfilled:
Sacramental confession, Eucharistic Communion and pray
for the intentions of the Pope (Our Father, Hail Mary and
Glory Be, as a minimum) with all your heart.

[FROM THE MANUAL OF INDULGENCES]

# Other works by the Author

These following videos are available on YouTube and on:
www.sremmanuel.org

- Devour the Book Which Tells the Truth! (27:44)
  With Sr. Emmanuel and her guest, Ralph Martin, NEW!
  (Don't miss to walk in God's Light in this time of confusion!)
  https://youtu.be/m9rQ7srO0E

- Stop, and Reflect on Your Future! (22:48) NEW!
  (An urgent appeal from Our Lady, as Eternity is at hand!)
  https://youtu.be/EmGrKCSw0Qw

- I Had an Appointment with Death at 5 pm.
  Sr. Emmanuel's Personal Testimony (37:00)
  https://www.youtube.com/watch?v=XYAub2cJWas&t=1s

- The Miracle Hidden in Your Rosary (21:12)
  https://www.youtube.com/watch?v=RCW36MwGl_c

- The Forgotten Power of Fasting (23:03)
  https://www.youtube.com/watch?v=g_FyRfrN6j4&t=243s

- Let Peace Flow to Your Heart Like a River (21:43)
  https://www.youtube.com/watch?v=4y5PCePDjgQ

- Come to Me! My Name is Mercy (34:59)
  https://www.youtube.com/watch?v=8fb-kOEcYQU

- Maïsa Arraf Sings in Arabic "Resurrection"(3:20)
  https://www.youtube.com/watch?v=-rfO8PrSvKo

- Paul, the Prayer of a Poor (13:31)
  https://www.youtube.com/watch?v=ffd0lVpzlEY

- Three Days to Defeat Death (37:54)
  https://www.youtube.com/watch?v=06gvD9k6wcU&t=264s

- Don't Miss Your Second Chance! Fr Daniele Natale (20:47)
  https://www.youtube.com/watch?v=aTxd-91pFpg

- The 24 Hours of the Gospa (12:150)
  https://www.youtube.com/watch?v=3SCyYoNqzwU

- Medjugorje in Confinement (4:36)
  https://www.youtube.com/watch?v=G5IsjZuFA-Q

- Consecrate Your Death and Heal from Fear (13:18)
  https://www.youtube.com/watch?v=xW5Nwq22FZY

- Choose Your Future; Heaven, Purgatory or Hell (25:18)
  https://www.youtube.com/watch?v=blbIte7VN4Q&t=152s

- Gratitude: the Secret to Happiness (13:43)
  https://www.youtube.com/watch?v=IXnL_MA92_A

- Sister Emmanuel Prays to Saint Joseph (13:37)
  https://www.youtube.com/watch?v=gummYHHoW44

- Forgive and be Free! (9:23)
  https://www.youtube.com/watch?v=do5c00glBKA

- Prayer to Jesus in the Womb of Mary (7:00)
  https://www.youtube.com/watch?v=RxqF5zk6ryI

- Jealousy: Commentary of Nov. 25 message, 2019 (6:24)
  https://www.youtube.com/watch?v=3cxAthNA78o

- The Chaplet of Divine Mercy (8:39)
  https://www.youtube.com/watch?v=FZa5DL05T-I

- You Had an Abortion? I have Something to Share with You! (4:50)
  https://www.youtube.com/watch?v=kncHijv_KLg

- The Power of Fasting in 10 minutes (9:26)
  https://www.youtube.com/watch?v=ROF6LxlVI_s

- Help Your Priests! (5:35)
  https://www.youtube.com/watch?v=LnbZJLuN0IM

- The Miracle of Baby Jesus (5:44)
  https://www.youtube.com/watch?v=9nPJv5tMByc

- How to Deal with Suffering (1:09:53)
  https://www.youtube.com/watch?v=Gg1AT7oy8R0

# Other books from the Author

- THE FORGOTTEN POWER
  OF FASTING
  Healing, Liberation, Joy . . .

"I READ YOUR BOOK FROM cover to cover. Your words completely captivated me and have convinced me on the importance of fasting. I knew already the benefits of fasting, but I wasn't aware of all its attributes, that you explain so well. Reading this book one discovers fasting.

As we know, Our Lady in Medjugorje continuously insists on the importance of fasting, but we avoid putting into practice something when it means we have to make a sacrifice. We struggle to convince ourselves to actually fast.

The arguments you present, and the examples that you give in this book, show very clearly the reason why Our Lady insists so persistently on something so precious for the soul and the body, for the apostolate on earth and for the souls in Purgatory. I thank you for emphasizing such an important topic, very often mentioned in Sacred Scripture, so precious for the living and for the intercession of the dead.

The final part of your work, with the words from the saints, will convince even the most reluctant.

This book will be nothing less than a true discovery of fasting to whoever reads it."

Don Gabriele Amorth

Euro 7.00

Sister Emmanuel

© 1995 Children of Medjugorje

www.sremmanuel.org

- CHILDREN, HELP MY HEART TO TRIUMPH!

AT THE HEIGHT OF THE BOS-nian War, Sister Emmanuel remained in Medjugorje with a few members of her community. During that time, memories of her father, a Prisoner of War during WWII, continually surfaced. Remembering how much he suffered, she felt a need to do something to spiritually help those on the front lines. Sister Emmanuel describes a call that she received at that time to appeal to the children for their sacrifices in order to alleviate the war. *Children, Help My*

*Heart To Triumph* was written in response to that call. It describes for children how to make a 9-day novena of little sacrifices. Included is a coloring book that they can color and mail to Medjugorje where they will be presented at one of Our Lady's apparitions.

US $ 11.99

Sister Emmanuel

© 1996 Children of Medjugorje

*Reprinted 2012 Includes Coloring Book*

www.sremmanuel.org

• THE AMAZING SECRET OF THE SOULS IN PURGATORY

IT IS NOT OFTEN THAT A BOOK touches the soul so deeply. *The Amazing Secret of the Souls in Purgatory* is such a book. Maria Simma, deceased in March of 2003, lived a humble life in the mountains of Austria. When she was twenty-five, Maria was graced with a very special charism—the charism of being visited by the many souls in Purgatory—and being able to communicate with them! Maria shares, in her own words, some amazing secrets about the souls in Purgatory.

She answers questions such as: What is Purgatory? How do souls get there? Who decides if a soul goes to Purgatory? How can we help get souls released from Purgatory?

US $ 8.99
© 1997 Queenship Publishing
www.queenship.org
www.sremmanuel.org

- THE HIDDEN CHILD
  OF MEDJUGORJE

"READING "MEDJUGORJE, THE 90s" had left me dazzled and so deeply touched that it had literally pulled me to Medjugorje. I just had to see with my own eyes the spiritual wonders retold in that book. Now with "The Hidden Child," the ember of love for Mary has received a new breath of air—a Pentecostal wind. Sr. Emmanuel is indeed one of Mary's best voices! Congratulations for this jewel of a testimonial! I wouldn't be surprised if the Gospa herself turned out to be Sister's most avid reader."

Msgr. Denis Croteau, OMI

"BOOKS ARE LIKE SEASHELLS; AT first they all look alike. However, they are far from being identical and their value varies greatly. Some of them are packed with riches and so well written, that they hide rare pearls within. Sister Emmanuel's book is one of those; it contains the most beautiful pearls, and with them enriches the reader. Through her accounts and anecdotes, the reader is pleased to meet people of great worth and to be filled with the teachings of so many events. Through this book, one will explore more fully a way still too little known: the way of the Queen of Peace."

Fr. Jozo Zovko, OFM

US $ 15.99
Sister Emmanuel
© 2010 Children of Medjugorje, Inc.
www.sremmanuel.org

---

- MARYAM OF BETHLEHEM, THE LITTLE ARAB

WHO IS THIS LITTLE ARAB? Maryam Baouardy is a daughter of Galilee. Her life? A succession of supernatural manifestations worthy of Catherine of Sienna. Maryam shares the keys of holiness, including ways to defeat Satan himself. This is a book you don't want to miss?

US $ 5.00
Sister Emmanuel
© 2012 Children of Medjugorje, Inc.
www.sremmanuel.org
*Available in E-Book*

---

- THE BEAUTIFUL STORY
  OF MEDJUGORJE
  As Told to Children
  from 7 to 97

IN THIS BOOK, YOU WILL FOL-
low the experiences of six little
shepherds, their shock when
they saw the "Lady" appearing
to them in 1981. You will see
how Vicka and Jokov actually
experienced the reality of life
beyond this world, when Our
Lady took them with her on
the most extraordinary journey
to Heaven, Purgatory and Hell.

You will learn how brave
they were under persecution.
You will be excited to know the
mes—sages they share from a

Mother who thinks only of
helping us, who loves each one
of us so much—including you
in a very special way!

You will read about the
powerful healings of bodies
and souls happening there, as
in Lourdes.

This is an adventure story,
except that this story is true
and is happening right now
for you!

US $5.00

Sister Emmanuel

© 2012 Children of Medjugorje

www.sremmanuel.org

*Available in E-Book*

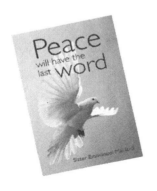

- PEACE WILL HAVE
  THE LAST WORD

THE MERCY OF GOD IS SCAN-
dalous, it even borders on the
extreme! In her engaging and
lively style, Sister Emmanuel
recounts real life stories and testimonies that take the reader's
heart on a journey of God's
mercy, passing through the
prisons of New York, and into
the confessionals of the Saints!

In these pages, a mosaic
of photos and parables, the
reader encounters the very
depths of the human heart
and is transported into the
midst of scenes and situations
that are as captivating as they
are diverse. Through them
we witness that much-desired
peace that comes from Above,
gaining victory over emptiness,
futility and fear.

Here are words that many
no longer dare to speak, and
yet, they have the power to
help rebuild a degenerating
society. This book is a shot in
the arm, an injection of hope
that will hasten the time when,
in the hearts of all, peace will
have the last word!

US $ 13.99
Sister Emmanuel
© 2015 Children of Medjugorje
www.sremmanuel.org

- SCANDALOUS MERCY
  When God Goes Beyond
  the Boundaries

WHY SCANDALOUS MERCY?

In these pages the reader will discover unexplored aspects of the Heart of God that you might think are crazy! Crazy with love! You will meet Mother Teresa, Maryam of Bethlehem, a Nazi criminal, a priest condemned to hell, a high ranking abortionist, a drug dealer from Brazil, a furious mother-in-law, a sick child . . . and in the middle of all this, the most beautiful Heart of Christ, who is calling ALL His children.

This beautiful selection of testimonies and "little flowers" picked from everyday life will capture the reader on two levels: first, the reader of this book will find his achy heart soothed and enriched by new ways to find hope in our difficult world today; second, he will be shocked to learn that these stories are true. They will make you laugh, cry, even tremble, but one thing is certain, they will all amaze you!

US $ 13.00
Sister Emmanuel
© 2015 Children of Medjugorje
www.sremmanuel.org

the miracles of Mary's motherly love.

- MEDJUGORJE, TRIUMPH
  OF THE HEART
  Revised Edition of
  Medjugorje of the 90s

SISTER EMMANUEL OFFERS A
pure echo of Medjugorje,
the eventful village where
the Mother of God has been
appearing since 1981. She
shares at length some of the
personal stories of the villagers, the visionaries, and the
pilgrims who flock there by
the thousands, receiving great
healings. Eight years of awe
have inspired this book. these
89 stories offer a glimpse into

Printed in Great Britain
by Amazon